Moving to California

Your guide to relocating to the Golden State

Alex Bugeja

Table of Contents

- **Introduction** - So You Want to Be a Californian, Eh? (Read This First, Seriously)

- **Chapter 1** The Rent is Too Damn High (and Other Housing Realities)

- **Chapter 2** Navigating the Freeways: A Crash Course (Pun Intended)

- **Chapter 3** Finding a Job That Pays More Than Your Avocado Toast Habit

- **Chapter 4** The DMV: Prepare for Your Spiritual Journey

- **Chapter 5** Earthquakes, Wildfires, and Other "Welcome Wagon" Gifts

- **Chapter 6** Understanding California Speak: From "Hella" to "The Industry"

- **Chapter 7** Picking Your Poison: NorCal vs. SoCal (The Eternal Struggle)

- **Chapter 8** Surfing, Hiking, or Just Sitting in Traffic: Choosing Your California Pastime

- **Chapter 9** The Cost of Living: It's Not a Myth, It's a Feature

- **Chapter 10** Recycling, Composting, and Judging Your Neighbors' Bins

- **Chapter 11** Dealing with Tourists (Bless Their Hearts)

- **Chapter 12** The Perils and Pleasures of California Cuisine (Beyond In-N-Out)

- **Chapter 13** Schools, Smog Checks, and Other Bureaucratic Hurdles

- **Chapter 14** Finding Your Tribe: From Tech Bros to Beach Bums

- **Chapter 15** Weekend Getaways: Deserts, Mountains, and Everything In Between

- **Chapter 16** Petiquette in the Golden State: Doggie Beaches and Organic Treats

- **Chapter 17** Health Insurance: Because That Urgent Care Bill Will Be Epic

- **Chapter 18** Utilities and Other Essential Adulting in California

- **Chapter 19** The California Dream vs. The California Reality: Managing Expectations

- **Chapter 20** Registering Your Car: Prepare for Paperwork Apocalypse

- **Chapter 21** The Great Outdoors: Avoiding Rattlesnakes and Poison Oak

- **Chapter 22** Joining the Cult: Fitness Trends and Wellness Obsessions

- **Chapter 23** Taxes, Taxes, and More Taxes (Welcome to the Club!)

- **Chapter 24** Learning to Love (or Tolerate) the Traffic Report

- **Chapter 25** Congratulations! You're (Almost) a Californian Now (Here's What's Next)

Introduction - So You Want to Be a Californian, Eh? (Read This First, Seriously)

Well, look at you. Standing on the precipice of a decision that countless hopefuls, dreamers, and the occasionally bewildered have made before you. You're thinking of moving to California. The Golden State. La La Land (parts of it, anyway). The place where ambitions soar as high as the rent, and the sunshine is only occasionally interrupted by an existential dread about traffic, earthquakes, or the price of a single avocado. Let's be honest, even entertaining this notion places you in a special category of optimistic, brave, or perhaps just sun-deprived individuals. Whatever your reasons – be it a career opportunity that sounds too good to be true (spoiler: check the cost of living chapter first), a desire to trade snow shovels for surfboards, or simply a lifelong dream fueled by Beach Boys songs and Hollywood fantasies – you're here. And since you've picked up this guide, you're at least smart enough to know that winging it might not be the best strategy when tackling a beast as beautiful and bewildering as California.

This isn't your grandma's guide to moving, bless her heart. We're not going to spend precious pages telling you how to pack a box (heavy stuff on the bottom, fragile stuff on top – you're welcome), or the importance of forwarding your mail (unless it's to warn you about the sheer volume of jury summonses you might now be eligible for). No, this guide assumes you've successfully navigated the basic human skill of relocating your worldly possessions from one abode to another within the grand tapestry of the United States of America. You know the drill: the questionable moving company quotes, the last-minute panic, the discovery of items you forgot you owned, and the solemn vow to become a minimalist (a vow that usually lasts until the first trip to IKEA in your new city).

Instead, we're diving headfirst into the glorious, frustrating, and utterly unique idiosyncrasies of becoming a Californian. This state, you see, isn't just another star on the flag; it's a whole different constellation. It plays by its own rules, speaks its own language (sometimes literally – looking at you, "hella"), and possesses a gravitational pull that can either launch you into the stratosphere or gently, persistently, grind you into a fine, sun-kissed powder. We're here to give you the unvarnished truth, the stuff the tourism brochures conveniently omit between panoramic shots of the Golden Gate Bridge and impossibly beautiful people laughing with salads. Think of us as that brutally honest friend who tells you there's spinach in your teeth, but for an entire state.

Why the special treatment? Because California, in its infinite variety and complexity, demands it. Moving here isn't just a change of address; it's an immersion into a culture, an economy, and an environment that can feel like another country, albeit one that still (mostly) uses the US dollar. From the fog-kissed avenues of San Francisco to the sun-drenched boulevards of Los Angeles, from the rugged majesty of the Sierras to the serene desolation of the Mojave, California offers a buffet of experiences so diverse it's a wonder it all fits within one state's borders. But with great diversity comes great... well, a great number of things to figure out.

Consider this your pre-location orientation, your "Welcome to the Jungle (Gym)" introductory course. We'll delve into the practical realities that often get glossed over in the sun-drenched narratives. We're talking about the kind of things that make you go "Huh?" or, more likely, "You have got to be kidding me." This includes navigating the housing market, which often feels like a high-stakes poker game where everyone else has a royal flush and you're holding a pair of twos and a grocery store loyalty card. We'll touch upon the legendary freeway system, a marvel of engineering that somehow manages to be both indispensable and the bane of everyone's existence. And yes, we will venture into the hallowed halls of the Department of Motor Vehicles, an experience so uniquely Californian it deserves its own epic poem (or at least a very long chapter).

This guide is also about the subtler aspects of assimilation. Understanding that "early" for a meeting in Los Angeles might mean "on time," while in San Francisco, it might mean "fashionably late by Silicon Valley standards." It's about realizing that your car is not just a mode of transport, but an extension of your living space, your dining room, and occasionally, your therapist's couch. It's about learning to discuss earthquake preparedness with the same casualness you once reserved for discussing the weather.

Now, for a very important, and we mean *very* important, piece of advice. Think of it as the fine print, the surgeon general's warning, the "read before operating heavy machinery" sticker for your California adventure: **Laws, regulations, fees, and official procedures in California can, and frequently do, change faster than a traffic light on a deserted street at 3 AM.** What's true today might be an amusing historical anecdote tomorrow. The cost of a vehicle registration, the rules for recycling your kombucha bottles, the exact decibel level your dog is allowed to bark at the mail carrier – these all subject to the whims of legislation and bureaucratic evolution.

Therefore, while we've sweated metaphorical blood to bring you the most current and relevant information possible at the time of writing, **this book is not a substitute for checking with official government sources.** Consider the websites for the State of California, your specific county, and your new city to be your new best friends. Bookmark them. Send them holiday cards. They will have the latest, greatest, and most legally binding information on everything you need to know. Think of this guide as your roadmap, but always, *always* check the official traffic conditions before you merge onto the highway. We're here to point you in the right direction, share some laughs, and maybe save you from a few rookie mistakes, not to provide definitive legal or financial counsel. That's what expensive professionals are for, and you'll find plenty of those in California too.

So, what can you expect from the following chapters? Prepare for a deep dive into the realities of California living, served with a side of wry humor and a dollop of "we've-been-there" empathy. We'll tackle the biggies: finding a place to live that doesn't require selling a kidney (Chapter 1), deciphering the cryptic dance of freeway driving (Chapter 2), and the eternal quest for gainful employment that can sustain your newfound appreciation for artisanal toast (Chapter 3). We'll guide you through the bureaucratic labyrinth that is the DMV (Chapter 4 – bring snacks for this one, both the chapter and the actual visit).

We'll also explore the unique environmental "welcoming committee" California has in store, from earthquakes to wildfires (Chapter 5), because knowing what to do when the ground starts doing the cha-cha is a surprisingly useful life skill here. You'll get a crash course in California lingo (Chapter 6), so you don't look completely bewildered when someone describes something as "gnarly" or asks if you're "cruising for a bruising." We'll even attempt to mediate the age-old NorCal vs. SoCal debate (Chapter 7), though we suspect that's a battle with no true victor, only deeply entrenched opinions.

From choosing your preferred method of communing with nature (or traffic, Chapter 8) to understanding why your paycheck seems to evaporate into thin air (Chapter 9, The Cost of Living: It's Not a Myth, It's a Feature), we're covering the bases. We'll even get into the nitty-gritty of trash – yes, trash – because in California, recycling and composting are practically competitive sports (Chapter 10). You'll learn strategies for dealing with the delightful, if sometimes overwhelming, influx of tourists (Chapter 11), and explore the culinary landscape that extends far beyond the siren song of In-N-Out Burger (Chapter 12).

Further down the rabbit hole, we'll navigate schools, smog checks, and other bureaucratic delights (Chapter 13), help you find your people, whether they're tech mavens or surfing savants (Chapter 14), and inspire your weekend wanderlust with getaway ideas (Chapter 15). For those bringing furry companions, we'll cover petiquette in the Golden State (Chapter 16), because Fido deserves the California dream too. We'll even broach the thrilling topics of health insurance (Chapter 17 – don't skip this, your appendix might thank you later), setting up utilities without losing your mind (Chapter 18), and the often-painful process of registering your out-of-state vehicle (Chapter 20 – brace for impact).

We'll also address the philosophical side of things, like managing the gap between the California Dream and the often-grittier California Reality (Chapter 19). We'll equip you for encounters with the state's less cuddly residents in the great outdoors (Chapter 21), give you a peek into the ever-evolving fitness and wellness scene (Chapter 22), and, because misery loves company, commiserate about taxes (Chapter 23). And just when you think you've got it all figured out, we'll discuss the art of learning to love, or at least stoically tolerate, the daily traffic report (Chapter 24).

What you *won't* find in this book is a generic checklist applicable to moving to Boise or Boca Raton. We're not here to tell you to rent a U-Haul, change your address with the post office, or say goodbye to your Aunt Mildred (though you probably should, she'll miss you). This is about the nuanced, often perplexing, and uniquely Californian aspects of your upcoming adventure. It's about the things that will make you laugh, cry, and possibly question your life choices, all within the span of a single Tuesday afternoon.

California has a way of challenging you, changing you, and, if you let it, charming the pants off you (sometimes literally, if you're not careful on a windy beach). It's a state of incredible contrasts: breathtaking natural beauty juxtaposed with mind-boggling urban sprawl; a culture of relentless innovation alongside a fierce determination to preserve its heritage; a land of laid-back vibes and high-strung ambitions. It's complicated, it's occasionally infuriating, and for many, it's undeniably magical.

So, take a deep breath. Maybe grab a stress ball (you'll find them useful later, particularly around Chapter 4 and Chapter 20). You're about to embark on a journey that's more than just a physical move. It's a transition, an education, and quite possibly, the beginning of a whole new chapter in your life story, hopefully one that doesn't involve too many parking tickets or encounters with particularly aggressive squirrels.

This guide is your companion for that journey. We can't promise it will all be easy – in fact, we can pretty much guarantee it won't be. But we can promise to share what we know, offer a few laughs along the way, and help you feel a little more prepared for the wild, wonderful, and utterly Californian experience that awaits. Welcome, almost, to the Golden State. Now, turn the page and let's get down to the brass tacks, or perhaps, the avocado pits.

CHAPTER ONE: The Rent is Too Damn High (and Other Housing Realities)

Alright, let's rip the Band-Aid off, shall we? You've seen the chapter title. You knew this was coming. If California were a theme park, the ride to find housing would be called "Wallet Whiplash Mountain," and the only souvenir you'd get is a significantly lighter bank account and a newfound appreciation for the concept of "cozy" (which, in California real estate lingo, often means "can you touch all four walls without moving your feet?"). Yes, the rent, in many desirable corners of this sun-kissed state, is indeed too damn high. It's so high, it's practically orbiting with the satellites, looking down on the rest of the country's rental markets with a smug, gold-plated sense of superiority.

Why, you ask, clutching your pearls and your budget spreadsheet? It's the classic California cocktail: one part relentless demand (everyone and their dog wants a piece of this sunshine), one part stubbornly limited supply (turns out, you can't just print more coastline or Silicon Valleys), a generous splash of complex zoning and building regulations that can make new construction feel like an archaeological dig, and a garnish of sheer, unadulterated desirability. People want to live here. They want the weather, the jobs, the beaches, the mountains, the vibe. And when demand outstrips supply like a Tesla out-accelerating a tricycle, prices tend to do what they do best: soar. It's not personal; it's just economics wearing a particularly expensive pair of sunglasses.

So, you're ready to dive into the shark-infested waters of the California rental market. Bless your optimistic heart. First things first: speed is of the essence. Good listings, especially in sought-after areas, disappear faster than free avocado samples at a farmers market. You'll need to be more prepared than a Boy Scout on a caffeine bender. This isn't just about casually browsing Zillow on a Sunday afternoon; this is a competitive sport. Get your documents in order *before* you even start looking: credit report (make sure it's shinier than a freshly waxed surfboard), proof of income (landlords will want to see you make at least three times the monthly rent, sometimes more), references from previous landlords (preferably ones who don't describe you as a "nightmare wrapped in human skin"), and a cover letter that could charm the pants off a hardened cynic. Think of it as your rental resume, designed to convince a skeptical landlord that you are, in fact, a responsible human being who won't clog the drains with quinoa or host unlicensed llama-themed raves.

The actual hunt will likely involve a multi-pronged attack. Online portals are your first port of call, but be warned: scammers love these sites as much as actual renters do. If a deal looks too good to be true (a three-bedroom beachfront bungalow in Malibu for $500 a month? Suuuuure), it absolutely, positively is. Some folks still swear by driving around neighborhoods looking for "For Rent" signs, a quaint throwback to a simpler time, like churning your own butter. This can occasionally unearth a hidden gem managed by an old-school landlord who hasn't quite embraced the digital age, but it's a bit like searching for a unicorn that also offers reasonable pet fees. Real estate agents or rental brokers can sometimes help, especially in high-density areas, but their fees will, naturally, add to the already eye-watering cost.

And then there are the open houses. Oh, the glorious, chaotic, occasionally soul-crushing open houses. In popular areas, these can resemble a casting call for a reality show titled "Desperate Renters." You'll see your competition sizing each other up, everyone trying to subtly impress the landlord or leasing agent while simultaneously trying to gauge if that weird stain on the carpet is a dealbreaker. Be prepared to fill out an application on the spot, sometimes on a clipboard balanced precariously on your knee, alongside twenty other hopefuls all vying for the same two-bedroom slice of heaven (or, more likely, a reasonably clean box with functioning plumbing).

Let's talk about deciphering rental listings. California landlords have developed a unique dialect. "Charming" and "cozy" almost invariably mean small. Really small. Like, "your bed might also be your dining table" small. "Vintage" or "historic character" can translate to "old, possibly with plumbing that predates the invention of the internet, and maybe a friendly ghost or two." "Rustic" often implies that you'll be doing some of the finishing work yourself, possibly with twigs and your own ingenuity. "Bright and airy" might mean there's one window that isn't painted shut. And if a listing screams "LOCATION, LOCATION, LOCATION!" in all caps, brace yourself for a broom closet in a trendy neighborhood, probably next to a very loud nightclub.

Square footage is another interesting concept. You'll see numbers that might make you think you're renting a walk-in closet for the price of a small castle in another state. It's crucial to see places in person if you can, because photos can be masters of illusion, making a shoebox look like a ballroom. And "utilities included" is a siren song. Clarify *exactly* which utilities. Water and trash are common, but electricity and gas? Less so. And in a state where air conditioning can be a non-negotiable necessity, that electricity bill can pack a punch.

The types of rental housing in California are as varied as the landscape. You've got your sprawling apartment complexes, often boasting amenities like pools (that you'll swear you'll use every day but probably won't) and fitness centers (ditto). These come with their own sets of rules, often lengthy and specific, covering everything from acceptable balcony decorations to the precise hours you're allowed to breathe too loudly. Then there are condos, owned by individuals but often located within larger communities governed by Homeowners Associations (HOAs). Renting a condo means you're not just beholden to your landlord, but also to the HOA's CC&Rs (Covenants, Conditions & Restrictions), which can dictate anything from the color of your window curtains to whether your emotional support peacock is welcome.

Single-family homes offer more privacy and often a yard (a patch of dirt you'll be expected to keep alive in a drought-prone state), but also more responsibility. Guess who's mowing that lawn or figuring out why the sprinklers are staging a reenactment of "Waterworld"? Usually, you. A growing trend, born out of necessity and changing regulations, is the ADU, or Accessory

Dwelling Unit. These are often converted garages, backyard cottages, or basement apartments. They can be a more affordable way to get into a desirable neighborhood, but be prepared for close proximity to your landlord, who might literally be living a few feet away, possibly judging your recycling habits.

And then there's the roommate situation. For a significant portion of Californians, especially in pricier urban areas, having roommates isn't just a quirky sitcom trope; it's a financial necessity well into adulthood. Finding compatible roommates is a whole other adventure, like online dating but with the added thrill of potentially sharing a bathroom with a stranger who has very different ideas about what constitutes "clean." Be prepared for conversations about shared chore wheels, quiet hours, and the passive-aggressive labeling of food in the refrigerator.

Now, let's wade into the murky waters of rent control. Yes, it exists in California. No, it's not a magical statewide shield protecting all renters from any and all rent increases. Rent control in California is a patchwork quilt of local ordinances. Some cities have it, some don't. Where it does exist, the rules vary wildly regarding which buildings are covered, how much rent can be increased annually, and what constitutes a "just cause" for eviction. The statewide Tenant Protection Act of 2019 (AB 1482) offered broader protections, but it also has its own set of exemptions and complexities. The takeaway? Don't assume you're covered. You absolutely *must* research the specific rent control and tenant protection laws for the city and county you're moving to. Official city or county housing websites are your best bet here.

Security deposits. Ah, that hefty chunk of change you hand over before you even get the keys, ostensibly to cover any damage you might inflict beyond normal wear and tear. In California, there are legal limits on how much a landlord can charge for a security deposit. For unfurnished units, it's typically up to two times the monthly rent; for furnished units, it can be up to three times. Getting it back at the end of your lease can sometimes feel like trying to extract a particularly stubborn tooth. Document everything. Take photos and videos of the unit's condition before you move in, noting every scratch, ding, and wonky doorknob. Do a thorough walk-through with your landlord upon moving out, if possible. Understand the difference between "normal wear and tear" (like lightly scuffed paint or worn carpet from walking) and "damage" (like a hole punched in the wall during an overly enthusiastic game of charades, or your artistic toddler's permanent marker mural).

The lease agreement. That intimidatingly thick stack of paper that you'll be tempted to just skim and sign. Don't. Read it. Every single word. This is a legally binding contract, and in California, leases can contain clauses specific to the state's unique proclivities. Look for sections on earthquake safety (you might receive a booklet), water conservation measures (California is often thirsty), pest control responsibilities (who pays if ants decide your kitchen is their new vacation home?), and mold disclosures or prevention guidelines. Many buildings now have strict no-smoking policies, not just inside units but on balconies and common areas too. And if you have a pet, or hope to get one, scrutinize the pet policy. Many landlords charge "pet rent," additional pet deposits, or have stringent restrictions on breed, size, or even the number of goldfish you can reasonably own.

The term "affordable" when discussing California housing is, shall we say, a highly relative concept. What passes for a king's ransom in one part of the country might get you a moderately spacious walk-in closet in San Francisco or Santa Monica. Costs do vary significantly across the state. You'll generally find lower rents in inland areas, the Central Valley, or more remote rural communities compared to the major coastal metropolises or tech hubs. But this often comes with trade-offs: longer commutes (see Chapter 2 for the joys of California traffic), fewer job opportunities in certain sectors, or a different pace of life and set of amenities. It's a balancing act, and only you can decide what compromises you're willing to make.

We should probably acknowledge the elephant in the room, or rather, the multi-million dollar mansion on the hill: buying a house. If you thought rents were high, wait until you peek at the for-sale listings in many California locales. The median home prices can make your eyes water and your financial planner weep. For many, especially newcomers, buying immediately is simply not on the table unless you're arriving with a Brinks truck full of cash or a winning lottery ticket. This chapter focuses on renting because, for a vast number of Californians, it's the reality, sometimes for many years. We're not saying homeownership is impossible, but it's a whole different level of financial commitment and market navigation, possibly requiring its own separate, and much scarier, book.

So, what's the secret to landing a rental in the Golden State without losing your mind or your life savings? There's no magic bullet, unfortunately. It often comes down to a potent cocktail of persistence (you will face rejection), preparedness (have those documents ready to go at a moment's notice), a flexible definition of "perfect," a healthy sense of humor (because sometimes you just have to laugh at the absurdity of paying so much for so little), and, let's be honest, a decent income. Being financially realistic about what you can truly afford is paramount. Don't stretch yourself so thin that you're eating instant noodles every night just to live in a trendy zip code, unless, of course, artisanal instant noodles are your passion.

Be prepared to make compromises. Your dream apartment with ocean views, a walk-in closet the size of a small European nation, and a landlord who bakes you cookies might not exist, or if it does, it's probably already rented to Beyoncé's second cousin. Maybe you sacrifice square footage for location, or a shorter commute for a slightly older building. Perhaps you embrace the roommate life for a few years. It's about finding the best possible fit within the often-constraining realities of the market.

Remember to trust your gut. If a landlord seems sketchy, or a building feels off, or the lease contains clauses that make your eyebrows shoot into your hairline, it's okay to walk away. There will be other listings, other opportunities. It might not feel like it when you're knee-deep in the search, but there will be. The process can be a marathon, not a sprint, so pace yourself and try not to get too discouraged by the inevitable bumps in the road.

Finding a place to live is often the biggest initial hurdle in the great California adventure. It can be stressful, expensive, and occasionally make you question why you ever thought this was a good idea. But once you clear that hurdle, once you have those keys in your hand and a place to call your own (even if it's a "cozy" one), you're one step closer to unpacking those boxes and starting to explore all the other weird and wonderful things this state has to offer. And who knows, maybe you'll even find a place with an avocado tree in the backyard. A Californian can dream, right?

CHAPTER TWO: Navigating the Freeways: A Crash Course (Pun Intended)

Welcome, brave traveler, to the circulatory system of California: the freeway. These sprawling networks of concrete and asphalt are the arteries and veins that pump life (and an astonishing number of vehicles) throughout the Golden State. To live here is to know them, to use them, and often, to curse them with a creativity you didn't know you possessed. Forget everything you *think* you know about highway driving from other, arguably more sedate, parts of the country. California freeways are a different beast, a high-speed ballet (or demolition derby, depending on the day) with its own unique choreography, unspoken rules, and local dialects.

First, let's talk names. In many parts of California, particularly Southern California, freeways are often referred to by a name *and* a number, and sometimes just "the" followed by the number. For example, you might hear someone say they're taking "the 405" (pronounced "the four-oh-five") or "the Hollywood Freeway" (which is a section of US-101). This "the" is a linguistic quirk that can immediately identify a Southern Californian. In Northern California, the "the" is less common, and people tend to just use the number (e.g., "80" or "101"). It might seem like a small detail, but get it wrong in conversation, and you might as well be wearing a sign that says "Fresh off the Turnip Truck." The historical reason for this often involved freeways initially having descriptive names before numbers became dominant, or a single freeway carrying multiple route numbers, making the name a simpler identifier.

Now, onto the actual driving experience. California's Basic Speed Law dictates that you may never drive faster than is safe for current conditions, regardless of the posted limit. The maximum speed limit on most California highways is 65 mph, though it can be 70 mph in some areas. On two-lane undivided highways, it's generally 55 mph. However, the *flow of traffic* is a powerful, often unwritten, rule. If you're in the far-left lane (often called the "fast lane") and traffic is moving at 75 mph, doing the posted 65 mph might earn you some unkind gestures, or worse, become a hazard. Conversely, driving significantly slower than the flow of traffic, even if you're at the speed limit, can also be dangerous and impede other vehicles. The key is to be predictable and aware.

Lane discipline is crucial. The left-most lane is generally intended for passing or for faster-moving traffic. If you're not actively passing, or if you're uncomfortable with the speed in that lane, move to a lane to your right. Slower traffic and vehicles towing trailers should typically stay in the right-hand lanes. Weaving in and out of lanes is generally frowned upon and can increase congestion and the risk of accidents.

And then there are carpool lanes, also known as High Occupancy Vehicle (HOV) lanes. These are usually the left-most lanes, marked with a diamond symbol. In Southern California, most HOV lanes require two or more occupants in the vehicle, 24/7. Some areas, like the El Monte Busway, may require three during peak hours. Northern California often has part-time HOV lanes, active only during peak commute times. Always check the posted signs for the specific requirements, as fines for violations can be hefty, often starting around $490. You can only enter and exit HOV lanes at designated points where there's a broken white line; crossing solid double lines is illegal. Motorcycles can typically use carpool lanes even with a single rider. Certain clean air vehicles (CAVs) with the proper DMV-issued decals may also qualify for HOV lane access with a single occupant, but rules can vary, so verify current regulations.

Some areas also feature High Occupancy Toll (HOT) lanes or Express Lanes. These allow solo drivers to use the carpool lane if they have an electronic toll collection device, commonly known as FasTrak, and pay a toll. Carpools may still use these lanes for free or a reduced toll, but often still require a FasTrak transponder, sometimes a specific "Flex" transponder where you can indicate the number of occupants. FasTrak is a statewide system, meaning a transponder from one California toll agency will work on all toll roads, bridges, and express lanes in the state.

Merging onto a California freeway can be an assertive act. You'll need to get up to the speed of freeway traffic in the acceleration lane before merging. Don't expect people to always make room for you; you need to find your opening and take it, safely but decisively. Using your turn signal is not just a suggestion; it's a necessity, though you'll quickly observe it's a frequently ignored one by some drivers. Always look over your shoulder to check your blind spots before changing lanes.

Exiting requires planning. Freeways here can have many lanes, and last-minute, multi-lane changes to reach an exit are dangerous and a hallmark of someone unfamiliar with their route. Know your exit in advance, and position yourself in the correct lane well ahead of time. Using a GPS app can be invaluable, especially in complex interchange areas.

One unique California phenomenon is motorcycle lane splitting. This is where motorcyclists ride between rows of stopped or slow-moving vehicles in the same lane. And yes, it's legal in California. The California Highway Patrol (CHP) offers safety guidelines for motorcyclists choosing to lane split, such as not exceeding the speed of other traffic by more than 10 mph and avoiding it when traffic is moving at 30 mph or faster. If you're driving a car, be aware of this practice. Check your mirrors and blind spots frequently, especially before changing lanes or when traffic slows. Intentionally blocking or impeding a motorcyclist is illegal.

You'll inevitably encounter the dreaded "SigAlert." Originally named after its inventor, Loyd Sigmon, a SigAlert is an official notification from the CHP about any unplanned event that closes at least one traffic lane for 30 minutes or more. This could be an accident, a spilled load, or any other incident causing significant disruption. When a SigAlert is issued, it's a good indicator that you're in for a long delay, and radio traffic reports and GPS apps will usually light up with the news.

Speaking of traffic reports, they are a way of life here. You'll hear them constantly on the radio, often giving estimates in "minutes of delay" rather than just speeds. Learning the local freeway names and numbers is key to understanding these reports. Many Californians rely heavily on real-time traffic apps like Google Maps or Waze to navigate and find alternative routes. Sometimes, surface streets (regular city roads) can be a viable, albeit slower, alternative during major freeway tie-ups.

Be prepared for a wide variety of road conditions and drivers. You'll encounter everything from meticulously maintained stretches of new pavement to older sections that are cracked and bumpy. Some freeways, particularly in urban areas, have grooved pavement. These longitudinal or transverse cuts in the concrete are designed to improve traction and reduce hydroplaning during wet weather by channeling water away. They can, however, sometimes make your car feel like it's "tramlining" or wiggling a bit, especially on motorcycles.

Aggressive drivers are, unfortunately, not uncommon. You'll see tailgating (driving too closely to the vehicle in front), sudden lane changes, and excessive speeding. The best defense is to maintain a safe following distance (the "three-second rule" is a good guideline), stay aware of your surroundings, and avoid engaging with aggressive drivers. Don't expect everyone to use their turn signals. It's a frustrating reality, so defensive driving is key.

Honking in California is generally perceived as a sign of aggression or a warning, not a friendly "hello" or "thank you." A quick tap on the horn might be used if someone is about to drift into your lane, but prolonged honking is usually a sign of impatience or anger.

If your vehicle becomes disabled on the freeway, try to pull over to the right shoulder as safely as possible. If you must exit your vehicle, do so from the right side, away from traffic. Stay in your vehicle with your seatbelt on if you can, and call 511 (the statewide traveler information service) or 911 for assistance. The CHP Freeway Service Patrol (FSP) provides free emergency roadside services in certain areas during commute times, like providing a gallon of gas or changing a flat tire.

Construction is a near-constant presence on California freeways. Be prepared for lane closures, detours, and reduced speed limits in work zones. Pay close attention to construction zone signs and be extra cautious around workers and equipment.

Certain freeways have reputations for being particularly challenging or dangerous due to high traffic volume, complex interchanges, or specific geographic hazards. For instance, I-5, which runs the length of the state, is known for heavy congestion in urban areas and significant truck traffic. The I-405 in Los Angeles is infamous for its gridlock. Mountain passes like I-80 through the Sierra Nevada or I-15 through the Cajon Pass can present challenges with weather (snow and ice in winter, high winds) and steep grades. Coastal routes like Highway 1 can be stunningly beautiful but also narrow and winding, requiring extra attention.

Rush hour in major metropolitan areas like Los Angeles, the San Francisco Bay Area, and San Diego can be an exercise in extreme patience. It often extends well beyond the traditional 9-to-5 window, with traffic sometimes building as early as 6 AM and lasting until 7 PM or later. Fridays can be particularly brutal, with getaway traffic starting early in the afternoon. If you have the flexibility, try to schedule your travel to avoid these peak times.

Finally, remember that California freeways are a shared space, used by millions of people every day. A little courtesy can go a long way. If someone signals to change lanes into your lane and there's space, letting them in (the "zipper merge" where appropriate) helps keep things flowing more smoothly. While the pace can be fast and the environment demanding, most Californians are just trying to get where they need to go, same as you.

Driving on California freeways is a skill honed over time. It requires alertness, a bit of assertiveness, and a healthy dose of situational awareness. It might seem intimidating at first, but with practice and by understanding the local norms, you'll be navigating "the 5," "the 101," or "the 880" like a seasoned local in no time. Just remember to breathe, stay calm, and maybe invest in a good audiobook library for those inevitable traffic jams.

CHAPTER THREE: Finding a Job That Pays More Than Your Avocado Toast Habit

So, you've braved the housing hunt (or are mentally preparing for that particular gauntlet) and you've begun to make peace with the idea of freeway combat. Excellent. Now, let's talk about the small matter of funding this California escapade. Unless you're arriving with a trust fund the size of a small nation's GDP or have a remarkable talent for monetizing your collection of vintage thimbles, you're going to need a job. And not just any job. You're going to need a job that generates enough income to keep the lights on, the landlord happy, and, yes, to occasionally indulge in that most Californian of culinary clichés: avocado toast, perhaps even with a fancy microgreen garnish.

The California job market, much like its freeways, is vast, varied, and can be intensely competitive. It's a land of opportunity, to be sure, but it's also a place where thousands of other bright-eyed and bushy-tailed individuals are vying for those same opportunities, often armed with impressive resumes and an unnerving tolerance for unpaid internships. The good news is that California boasts one of the largest and most diverse economies in the world. The less good news is that you'll need to be strategic, persistent, and perhaps a little bit lucky to land the gig that justifies the sunshine tax.

Let's start with the big hitters, the industries that make California's economic heart beat. First up, the undisputed heavyweight champion: **Tech**. You've heard of Silicon Valley (stretching roughly from South San Francisco down to San Jose), the global epicenter of innovation, questionable billionaires, and company campuses that look more like futuristic amusement parks. If you're in software engineering, data science, AI, cybersecurity, or pretty much anything involving bits and bytes, this is your Mecca. But the tech scene isn't confined to the Bay Area. "Silicon Beach" in Los Angeles (Santa Monica, Venice, Playa Vista) is a major hub, as are parts of San Diego and even Sacramento. The roles are plentiful, the salaries can be eye-popping, and the perks often include free food, on-site gyms, and the existential dread of wondering if your startup will still exist in six months.

Then there's **Entertainment**, "The Industry," primarily centered in Los Angeles but with tendrils reaching throughout Southern California. This isn't just about becoming the next movie star (though if that's your dream, good luck and may the odds be ever in your favor). It's a massive ecosystem encompassing film and television production, music, gaming, digital media, and all the supporting roles that make the magic happen – from gaffers and grips to agents, publicists, and studio accountants. Breaking in can be notoriously difficult, often relying on who you know and a willingness to start at the bottom, possibly fetching coffee for someone who fetches coffee for someone important.

Lest you think California is all glamour and algorithms, let's not forget **Agriculture**. The Central Valley is one of the most productive agricultural regions on the planet, feeding a significant portion of the country and beyond. While perhaps not as glitzy as Hollywood, agriculture and its related industries (food processing, logistics, agricultural technology or "AgTech") provide a massive number of jobs. If your skills lie in agribusiness, crop science, or managing large-scale farming operations, this fertile crescent could be your promised land. Expect less traffic than LA, but perhaps more passionate discussions about water rights.

Tourism and Hospitality are, naturally, colossal employers in a state that attracts visitors like moths to a very expensive, very sunny flame. From the iconic theme parks of Anaheim and Valencia to the wineries of Napa and Sonoma, the ski resorts of the Sierras, and the countless hotels, restaurants, and attractions up and down the coast, opportunities abound. These roles often require a sunny disposition (even when dealing with a tourist who can't find the Hollywood sign) and can range from entry-level service positions to high-level management in luxury resorts.

Don't overlook **Biotechnology and Life Sciences**. The San Francisco Bay Area and San Diego are global leaders in this field, with numerous pharmaceutical companies, research institutions, and biotech startups. If you've got a PhD in molecular biology or experience in clinical trials, these innovation clusters will be calling your name. The work is often cutting-edge, and the potential to make a real difference is immense, though you might need a PhD just to understand the coffee machine instructions in some labs.

Aerospace has a long and storied history in California, particularly in Southern California. While not the behemoth it once was during the Cold War, it remains a significant industry, with companies involved in aircraft manufacturing, space exploration (yes, rocket science is still a thing here), and defense contracting. If you're an engineer with a penchant for things that fly very fast or very far, there are still plenty of opportunities to reach for the stars, or at least a well-paying government contract.

Contrary to popular belief, things are still actually *made* in California. **Manufacturing** has evolved, with a focus on high-tech goods, electronics, and specialized products. Areas like the Inland Empire and parts of Los Angeles County have significant manufacturing sectors. And let's not forget the burgeoning electric vehicle (EV) manufacturing scene, which is putting a modern spin on California's automotive history.

Of course, with so many people living and working here, **Healthcare** is a perpetually robust sector. Nurses, doctors, medical technicians, hospital administrators, and a vast array of allied health professionals are in constant demand across the state. If you're in the medical field, you'll find opportunities in sprawling hospital networks, private practices, and specialized clinics from Eureka to El Centro.

And let's not forget the public sector. **Government** (state, county, and city) and **Education** (from K-12 to the vast University of California and California State University systems) are enormous employers. These jobs often come with good benefits and a level of stability that can be appealing, though navigating the bureaucracy of a government hiring process might require the patience of a saint who also happens to be a qualified project manager.

Now, how does one actually snag one of these coveted California jobs? Well, the usual suspects apply: a polished resume, a killer cover letter, and the ability to string coherent sentences together in an interview. But California has its own quirks. **Networking** here isn't just a good idea; it's practically a competitive sport. In a state where personal connections can open doors faster than a universal remote, attending industry meetups, conferences, alumni events, or even just striking up conversations at your local dog park (a surprisingly effective networking venue) can be invaluable. Californians, despite their sometimes-frenetic pace, can be surprisingly open to connecting if you approach it genuinely.

While general job boards like Indeed and LinkedIn are essential, don't neglect **niche sites** specific to your industry. There are tech-focused boards, entertainment industry job listings, academic job portals, and so on. Sometimes the best opportunities are found on these more specialized platforms. **Recruiters** can also be a valuable asset, particularly in fields like tech and healthcare. A good recruiter can be your advocate and guide, though remember they ultimately work for the company doing the hiring. Do your research and find recruiters who specialize in your field and have a good reputation.

The **California interview** can be a unique experience. In many industries, particularly tech and creative fields, there's a veneer of "California Casual." You might see interviewers in jeans and hoodies. However, don't let this fool you into thinking you can show up in your pajamas (unless you're interviewing for a mattress testing position, maybe). "Business casual" is usually a safe bet, but always err on the side of slightly more formal if you're unsure, especially in more traditional sectors like finance or law. The questions might be less about your five-year plan and more about your problem-solving skills, your ability to collaborate, and whether you'd be a "good fit" for the company culture, which can sometimes be an enigmatic concept.

One question that often plagues out-of-state applicants is whether they need a **local California address** on their resume. While it's becoming less of an issue with the rise of remote interviews, some old-school hiring managers might still consciously or unconsciously favor local candidates, assuming they can start sooner or are more committed to staying. If you have friends or family in California whose address you can *legitimately* use (with their explicit permission, of course, and only if you genuinely plan to be there for interviews), it might give you a slight edge in some cases. Otherwise, be prepared to explain your relocation plans and timeline clearly.

Speaking of relocation, the **remote work** landscape in California has exploded, just like everywhere else, but with a Californian twist. Many tech companies have embraced remote or hybrid models, which can be a game-changer if you dream of living in a slightly more affordable part of the state (or even a different state, though that comes with tax implications we'll touch on later) while still working for a California-based company. However, "remote" doesn't always mean "work from anywhere in a van down by the river." Companies often have policies about which states you can work from, so clarify those details.

Now, let's talk about the green stuff, the moolah, the cheddar – your **salary**. You'll see job postings with salaries that might look incredibly high compared to what you're used to. Before you start mentally furnishing your Malibu beach house, remember Chapter One: The Rent is Too Damn High. California salaries are often inflated to account for the astronomical cost of living, particularly in coastal cities and tech hubs. That six-figure salary might sound impressive, but after factoring in rent, taxes, and the $7 latte that's somehow become a daily necessity, you might find your disposable income isn't quite what you envisioned. Use online cost-of-living calculators to compare your current city with your target California location and get a realistic picture of what salary you'll actually need to maintain or improve your standard of living.

When it comes to **negotiating your salary**, don't be shy. Given the high cost of living, there's often an expectation that you will negotiate. Do your research on average salaries for your role and experience level in that specific California region (salaries can vary significantly even within the state). Be prepared to articulate your value and why you deserve the salary you're asking for. Also, look beyond the base salary. **Benefits packages** are crucial. California has certain state-mandated benefits, like paid sick leave, but company offerings can vary wildly. Look for comprehensive health insurance (you'll thank us when you read Chapter 17), generous paid time off (you'll want to explore all that California sunshine, after all), retirement savings plans, and, in the tech world, the allure of stock options or RSUs (Restricted Stock Units), which could be worth a fortune… or absolutely nothing.

It's also worth familiarizing yourself with some basics of **California labor law**. The state generally has more employee-friendly regulations than many other parts of the country. This includes rules around overtime pay (generally after 8 hours in a day or 40 in a week for non-exempt employees), mandatory meal and rest breaks, and protections against wrongful termination. Again, the official website for the California Department of Industrial Relations is your friend for the most accurate and up-to-date information. Don't rely on what your cousin's friend who once visited California told you.

For those with an entrepreneurial spirit or a desire for more flexibility, California is a massive hub for the **gig economy and freelance life**. Creative professionals, IT consultants, writers, designers, and even dog walkers can often carve out a living by piecing together various projects. The allure of being your own boss and setting your own hours is strong, especially in a state that values individualism. However, the freelance life comes with its own set of challenges: inconsistent income streams, the need to constantly hustle for new work, paying for your own health insurance, and the joys of self-employment taxes (a topic that will get its own thrilling spotlight in Chapter 23).

California has also been at the forefront of the debate around worker classification, most notably with Assembly Bill 5 (AB5), which aimed to reclassify many independent contractors as employees, entitling them to benefits and protections. The law has been controversial and has seen various amendments and legal challenges, particularly for certain professions. If you're planning to work as an independent contractor in California, it's absolutely critical to understand the current legal landscape regarding worker classification, as it can significantly impact your tax obligations and legal standing. This is definitely an area where checking official state resources or consulting with a legal professional is advisable.

Don't forget that California is a huge state, and job markets can vary significantly by region. The opportunities in **NorCal** (dominated by tech in the Bay Area, government in Sacramento, and agriculture in the Central Valley) can look quite different from those in **SoCal** (with its entertainment focus in LA, biotech in San Diego, and logistics in the Inland Empire). Even within these broad regions, there are nuances. Do your research on the specific industries and employers in the cities or areas you're considering. Sometimes, looking beyond the most obvious, most expensive metropolises can uncover hidden gem job markets with a more manageable cost of living. Consider cities in the Central Valley, the Inland Empire, or even more northern parts of the state if your industry has a presence there.

There's often a tension in California between pursuing a **passion** and earning a **paycheck** big enough to survive. The state attracts dreamers, artists, and innovators who are passionate about their work. But passion doesn't pay the rent for that "cozy" studio apartment. Finding a job that offers both personal fulfillment and financial stability is the holy grail. Sometimes, it might mean taking a "survival job" while you work towards your dream career, or finding creative ways to combine your passions with marketable skills. Don't feel like a sellout if your first job in California is more about paying the bills than changing the world. Many successful Californians started that way.

Finding a job in California can feel like a full-time job in itself. It requires research, dedication, networking savvy, and the ability to handle rejection without dissolving into a puddle of despair. The competition is fierce, the standards can be high, and the sheer scale of it all can be daunting. But every day, people from all over the country and the world successfully navigate this process and land fulfilling jobs that allow them to build a life in the Golden State.

So, polish that resume until it shines brighter than a newly detailed Tesla. Practice your elevator pitch until you can recite it in your sleep (which you might be doing a lot of, if you're stressed about the job hunt). Dive into the networking scene with the enthusiasm of a golden retriever at a squirrel convention. It might take time, it might take a few false starts, and it will almost certainly require more effort than you initially anticipate. But the reward – a job that not only supports your California adventure but also, ideally, makes you excited to get out of bed in the morning (even if it's into traffic) – is well worth the effort. And yes, with the right gig, you'll definitely be able to afford that avocado toast. Maybe even with a side of locally sourced, organically grown, artisanally crafted existential satisfaction.

CHAPTER FOUR: The DMV: Prepare for Your Spiritual Journey

Ah, the California Department of Motor Vehicles. The DMV. Just uttering the acronym can evoke a Pavlovian cocktail of emotions in seasoned Californians: a frisson of dread, a nostalgic twinge for hours of life they'll never get back, and perhaps, a perverse sense of pride for having survived its labyrinthine processes. If you're new to the Golden State, or soon to be, consider your upcoming interactions with the DMV not merely as bureaucratic errands, but as a profound rite of passage, a spiritual pilgrimage that will test your patience, your resolve, and quite possibly, your eyesight under fluorescent lighting. This isn't just about getting a plastic card with your picture on it; it's about earning your Californian stripes, one numbered ticket and bewildering form at a time.

Forget any preconceived notions you might have from DMVs in other, lesser states. The California DMV operates on a scale and with a certain élan that is uniquely its own. It's the keeper of keys to many Californian kingdoms: your driver's license, your state identification card, and the sacred scrolls pertaining to your vehicle's legal right to roam the freeways (though we'll delve deeper into the specific joys of vehicle registration in Chapter 20 – consider this chapter your warm-up act for that particular circus).

Before we embark on this enlightening journey, let us pause for the obligatory, yet critically important, mantra: **The California DMV website is your sacred text.** Rules, regulations, required documents, fees, office hours, and appointment procedures can and do change. They change with the wind, with the tides, with the legislative session. What you read here is a guide to the general experience, the lay of the land, the emotional landscape. For the absolute, up-to-the-minute, legally binding truth, thou shalt consult www.dmv.ca.gov. Bookmark it. Memorize it. Perhaps even make it your homepage for a while. You'll be visiting it more often than your favorite cat video website.

Now, steel your nerves, pack your metaphorical trail mix, and let's discuss how one begins this pilgrimage. In olden times (say, a few years ago), walking into a DMV office without an appointment was an act of heroic folly, a gamble worthy of a Vegas high roller, but with much lower odds of a satisfactory outcome. Today, while appointments are still the golden ticket to a more predictable (though not necessarily swift) experience, the DMV has made strides in managing the masses. Still, an appointment is your best friend. These coveted time slots are typically booked online or by phone. Be prepared for a bit of a digital quest. Popular offices in urban areas can have appointments booked out for weeks, sometimes months. The key is persistence and flexibility. Try checking for openings early in the morning or late at night when new slots might be released. Consider looking at DMV offices in slightly less populated nearby areas if your local branch looks like it's booking into the next geological epoch.

What if you're feeling brave, or an urgent need arises and appointments are scarce? You *can* attempt a walk-in visit. If you choose this path of the warrior, arrive early. No, earlier than that. Think "before the birds are entirely sure it's morning" early. You'll likely join a queue that snakes around the building, a silent, hopeful testament to shared human endurance. Bring water, a snack, and perhaps a compelling novel, because you're going to be there for a while. Some DMV locations have separate lines for appointments and walk-ins, so make sure you're in the correct one, lest you incur the silent wrath of your fellow pilgrims.

California has also been expanding its network of DMV Now kiosks. These self-service terminals, often found in DMV offices and even some grocery stores or public libraries, can handle a surprising number of transactions, like vehicle registration renewal or submitting proof of insurance. If your task is simple and kiosk-eligible, this can be a miraculous time-saver. Additionally, the American Automobile Association (AAA) offers some DMV services to its members at select offices, primarily related to vehicle registration and title transfers. This can be a significantly more pleasant experience, but it's for members only and doesn't cover driver's license applications or testing. And, of course, the

DMV website itself allows you to complete many tasks online, so always check there first to see if you can avoid an in-person visit altogether.

Once your appointment is secured, or you've committed to the walk-in adventure, the next crucial phase is the gathering of your sacred texts: the documentation. This is where many a hopeful Californian has stumbled. The DMV is understandably particular about proving you are who you say you are and that you actually live where you claim to live. For a new California driver's license or ID card, especially a REAL ID, the requirements are specific and non-negotiable.

The REAL ID is a federally compliant driver's license or ID card that will be required to board domestic flights and enter secure federal facilities. If you're going through the trouble of getting a California license, you'll almost certainly want to make it a REAL ID. This means you'll need to provide:

1. **Proof of Identity:** An original or certified copy of a birth certificate, a valid U.S. passport, permanent resident card, etc. Photocopies are generally a no-go.

2. **Proof of Social Security Number:** Your Social Security card, a W-2 form, or a paystub with your full SSN. Again, originals are usually required.

3. **Two Proofs of California Residency:** This is where it gets interesting. You'll need two different documents from an approved list, showing your name and current California address. Think utility bills (gas, electric, water, internet – but not your mobile phone bill, usually), rental or lease agreements, mortgage statements, bank statements, or official government mail. The names on these documents must match the name on your identity document. Make sure these are recent!

Again, and we cannot stress this enough, **consult the DMV website for the most current and comprehensive list of**

acceptable documents for the REAL ID. The list is specific. Bringing a heartfelt plea and a library card won't cut it. The feeling of arriving at the DMV after a lengthy wait, only to be turned away because your second proof of residency is a love letter from your landlord instead of a gas bill, is a uniquely Californian form of despair. Organize your documents meticulously. Make a checklist. Double-check it. Then, have a friend check it.

You've made it! You have an appointment (or heroic levels of patience), your documents are in order, and you're standing at the threshold of a California DMV field office. Take a deep breath. The ambiance is usually a delightful mix of institutional beige, the gentle hum of fluorescent lights, and the collective murmur of anxious anticipation. There will be lines. There will be forms. There will be people from every walk of life, united by the common goal of escaping with their sanity and the correct piece of paper.

If you have an appointment, there might be a specific check-in line or procedure. If you're a walk-in, you'll likely be directed to a general information or "start here" line, where a DMV employee will assess your needs and give you a numbered ticket or direct you to the next appropriate queue. This numbered ticket is your new best friend and your temporary identity. Guard it with your life. Listen for your number to be called or watch the display screens like a hawk. The moment your number flashes, or is announced over a loudspeaker system that may or may not sound like it was salvaged from a World War II submarine, is a moment of pure, unadulterated hope.

The waiting period can range from "surprisingly quick" (a rare and beautiful unicorn) to "I think I just aged a year." This is where your preparation pays off. That book, that fully charged phone (perhaps with headphones, to be courteous), those emergency snacks – they are your allies. Observe the ebb and flow, the fascinating tapestry of humanity. You might even strike up a conversation with a fellow traveler on this bureaucratic odyssey. Misery, after all, loves company.

When your number is finally called, approach the designated window with your documents neatly organized and a pleasant demeanor. Remember, DMV employees are people too. They deal with an endless stream of customers, some of whom are understandably stressed or confused. A little politeness and preparedness on your part can go a long way toward a smoother transaction. Have your forms filled out as completely as possible beforehand (many are available for download on the DMV website). Listen carefully to their instructions. Answer their questions clearly.

Now, for the trials and tribulations, otherwise known as the tests. First up is usually the **vision test**. It's a fairly standard affair. If you wear glasses or contact lenses for driving, make sure you have them with you. The ability to distinguish fuzzy letters from slightly less fuzzy letters is paramount.

Next, for those applying for a new license or, in many cases, renewing one, comes the **knowledge test**, often referred to as the written test. Do not underestimate this. The California Driver Handbook is your study guide. Read it. Internalize it. It's not just about traffic signs and speed limits; it's about understanding California's specific rules of the road. Things like the nuances of right turns on a red light (generally permitted after a full stop, unless a sign says otherwise), the strict laws regarding pedestrian right-of-way in crosswalks (marked or unmarked), the intricacies of HOV lane usage, and the different speed limits for various types of roads and vehicles. The test is typically administered on a touchscreen computer and is available in multiple languages. If you fail, don't despair. You usually get a certain number of attempts (often three) within your application period, though there might be a short waiting period before you can retake it. The questions are designed to ensure you have a grasp of the rules that keep California's roads (somewhat) orderly.

If you're a brand-new driver, or if your out-of-state license has long since expired, you'll also face the **driving test**, also known as the behind-the-wheel test. Scheduling this can be another adventure in appointment hunting. On the day of your test, you'll need to provide a vehicle that is in good working order (working signals, horn, brake lights, safe tires, etc.) and properly insured and registered. The examiner will perform a pre-drive safety check on your vehicle. If your car fails this initial inspection (e.g., a brake light is out), your test may be canceled on the spot.

During the driving test, the examiner will be evaluating your ability to safely operate a vehicle according to California law and good driving practices. They'll be looking for things like smooth acceleration and braking, proper lane positioning, correct use of signals, scanning your surroundings (checking mirrors and blind spots frequently – they *really* look for this), speed control, and your ability to follow directions. There are certain "critical driving errors" that can result in an automatic fail, such as running a red light, failing to yield right-of-way, or striking an object. Try to stay calm and focused. Nerves are normal, but a complete meltdown isn't going to help. At the end, the examiner will let you know if you've passed or failed and will usually provide some feedback.

Once you've navigated the tests, it's time for fees and photos. The DMV charges various fees for applications, licenses, and tests. Check the website for current fee amounts and acceptable forms of payment. They usually take cash, checks, money orders, and debit/credit cards, but it's always wise to confirm.

And then, the moment of truth: the DMV photo. This picture will be with you for years, silently judging your fashion choices from the depths of your wallet. While you won't have a Hollywood glam squad on hand, you can at least try to look presentable. Maybe don't roll out of bed and go straight there after an all-night study session fueled by questionable energy drinks. A quick comb of the hair, a reasonably clean shirt – small efforts can make a big difference between "acceptable human" and "escaped cryptid."

If you've successfully completed all requirements and passed your tests, you'll typically receive an interim license or ID card, which is a paper document valid for a short period (usually 60-90 days). Your permanent, REAL ID compliant card will be mailed to you.

The DMV will give you an estimate of when to expect it, but patience is, once again, a virtue.

There are a few California-specific considerations to keep in mind. If you are a **new California resident** and plan to drive, you are required to apply for a California driver's license within **10 days** of establishing residency. "Residency" can be established in several ways, including being employed in California, renting or buying a home, or enrolling your children in a California school. Don't delay this; driving on an out-of-state license beyond this grace period could cause you problems if you're pulled over.

If you have a valid **out-of-state driver's license**, the process to transfer it to California usually involves surrendering your old license, providing all the necessary REAL ID documentation, passing the vision test, and passing the knowledge test. The driving test is often waived if your out-of-state license is still valid or only recently expired, but the DMV reserves the right to require it.

Getting a **motorcycle license** involves specific written and riding skill tests. If you're aiming for a **Commercial Driver's License (CDL)** to operate large trucks or buses, prepare for a significantly more rigorous and complex process, with federal regulations playing a large role. One helpful service often offered at the DMV is **voter registration**, as part of the "Motor Voter" program, allowing you to register to vote when you apply for or renew your license.

Surviving your DMV experience is a significant milestone in your California journey. There will be moments of frustration, perhaps even bewilderment. You might question the very fabric of bureaucracy. But when you finally walk out, interim license in hand, there's a genuine sense of accomplishment. You've faced the beast and emerged, if not entirely unscathed, at least victorious.

Remember to treat the entire process with a sense of detached amusement where possible. Laugh at the absurdity. Commiserate with your fellow applicants. And above all, be prepared. The

California DMV is not a casual undertaking. It's a crucible that forges patience, resilience, and an encyclopedic knowledge of acceptable residency documents. Once you have that shiny new California license, you're one step closer to becoming a true Californian, ready to tackle the freeways and perhaps, just perhaps, even afford that avocado toast you've been dreaming about. And don't worry, you'll get to experience the magic all over again for renewals, or when it's time to register your vehicle – but that's a story for another chapter.

CHAPTER FIVE: Earthquakes, Wildfires, and Other "Welcome Wagon" Gifts

Alright, you've started to wrap your head around the housing tango, the freeway ballet, and the job market hustle. Feeling pretty good, are you? Ready to kick back with that hard-earned avocado toast? Excellent. Now, allow us to introduce you to California's more… *elemental* forms of entertainment. Think of them as the state's very own, occasionally overzealous, welcome wagon, bearing gifts that can range from a gentle shimmy of the floorboards to skies the color of a Martian sunset. We're talking, of course, about earthquakes, wildfires, and a few other natural phenomena that like to keep Californians on their toes, or occasionally, under their sturdy tables.

Don't panic. Millions of people live perfectly happy, long, and relatively unshaken (or un-singed) lives here. But ignoring these potential party crashers is like ignoring the "check engine" light on that vintage convertible you just bought to cruise PCH. It's all part of the California experience package, and being prepared is not just smart; it's practically a local pastime, right up there with complaining about traffic and debating the merits of various juice cleanses. Consider this chapter your introductory seminar to "Advanced Californian Environmental Awareness."

First up, the one that gets all the press: **earthquakes**. Yes, California is colloquially known as "Shakeyville" for a reason. The state is crisscrossed by a veritable spiderweb of fault lines, the most famous being the San Andreas Fault, a geological superstar with its own PR team (mostly seismologists and worried newscasters). These faults are where tectonic plates, those giant puzzle pieces that make up the Earth's crust, like to have arguments. When they slip or grind against each other, the ground shakes. Sometimes it's a tiny, almost imperceptible tremor that makes you wonder if the neighbor's washing machine is on the fritz. Other times, it's a more pronounced jolt that sends your knick-knacks skittering and your heart into your throat. And very, very rarely, it's "The Big One" that disaster movies love to depict.

The good news is that most earthquakes in California are minor. You'll feel a little wobble, the dog might look confused, and your East Coast relatives will immediately call in a panic after seeing it on the news, even if you barely noticed. However, the potential for a larger, more damaging quake is always there. It's not a matter of *if*, say the geologists with their knowing, slightly unnerving smiles, but *when*. This isn't meant to induce sleepless nights, but rather to underscore the importance of being prepared.

So, what does being an earthquake-savvy Californian entail? First, the mantra: **"Drop, Cover, and Hold On."** When the shaking starts, do not run outside (falling debris is a major hazard). Instead:

- **DROP** to your hands and knees. This position prevents you from being knocked down and allows you to crawl to shelter.

- **COVER** your head and neck (and your entire body if possible) under a sturdy table or desk. If there's no shelter nearby, get down near an interior wall (away from windows, bookcases, or tall furniture that could fall on you) and cover your head and neck with your arms.

- **HOLD ON** to your shelter (or to your head and neck) until the shaking stops. Be prepared for aftershocks, which can follow the main quake.

Next, let's talk about your **earthquake kit**. This isn't just for hardcore preppers; it's a basic household essential in quake country. Think of it as a "break glass in case of emergency" box, but for when the glass is already breaking. You'll want:

- **Water:** At least one gallon per person per day, for several days.

- **Food:** Non-perishable, ready-to-eat items (canned goods, energy bars, dried fruit). Don't forget a manual can opener!

- **First-aid kit:** A comprehensive one, plus any personal medications.

- **Flashlight:** With extra batteries. Don't rely on your phone; save its battery for communication.

- **Battery-powered or hand-crank radio:** For staying informed if power and internet are out. A NOAA Weather Radio is even better.

- **Whistle:** To signal for help.

- **Dust mask:** To help filter contaminated air.

- **Plastic sheeting and duct tape:** For sheltering-in-place, if needed.

- **Wrench or pliers:** To turn off utilities (gas and water) if necessary. Know where your shut-off valves are *before* you need them.

- **Local maps:** In case GPS is down.

- **Chargers and a backup battery/power bank:** For your cell phone.

Keep this kit in an easily accessible place. Some people keep smaller kits in their cars and at work too. It's better to have it and not need it than to need it and be rummaging through a debris-filled garage in the dark.

Beyond the kit, there's **home preparedness**. Look around your home with "earthquake eyes." What could fall and hurt someone or break?

- **Secure heavy furniture:** Bookshelves, mirrors, and tall dressers can be anchored to wall studs.

41

- **Secure your water heater:** Strapping it to the wall studs can prevent it from falling, rupturing, and causing a flood or gas leak. This is often required by code.

- **Store heavy and breakable items on lower shelves.**

- **Use museum putty or quake wax** to secure fragile items on display.

- **Check your home's foundation.** If you're buying a home, especially an older one, a seismic retrofitting evaluation might be a wise investment. Renters should ask their landlords about any seismic safety measures taken in the building.

Now, a word about **earthquake insurance**. It's typically not included in standard homeowners or renters insurance policies in California; it's a separate policy you have to purchase. It can be expensive, and deductibles are often quite high (usually a percentage of the home's replacement value, like 10-20%). Whether it's worth it depends on your financial situation, your risk tolerance, and the construction of your home. The California Earthquake Authority (CEA) is a publicly managed, not-for-profit provider of earthquake insurance. Get quotes, understand what's covered (and what's not), and make an informed decision.

After the shaking stops, be cautious. Check for injuries. Check for damage to your home – cracks in the foundation or walls, leaning structures. If you smell gas or see sparks, get out and call the utility company from a safe distance. Be prepared for power outages and disruptions to water and sewer services.

Official resources like the United States Geological Survey (USGS) website and the California Governor's Office of Emergency Services (CalOES) provide invaluable information, real-time quake maps, and preparedness guides. Many counties and cities also have their own emergency management offices with local resources. Familiarize yourself with these. Being informed is your best defense against becoming an uninformed casualty.

Now, let's shift our gaze from the ground beneath our feet to the skies above, which can, on occasion, take on an unsettling orange hue. We're talking about **wildfires**. California's stunning landscapes, with their vast forests, chaparral-covered hillsides, and grassy plains, are, unfortunately, also prime real estate for flames, especially during dry, windy conditions. What used to be a somewhat predictable "fire season" (typically late summer and fall) has, in recent years, felt more like a year-round anxiety in many parts of the state, fueled by drought, climate change, and sometimes, tragically, human carelessness.

If you're planning to live in or near what's known as the Wildland-Urban Interface (WUI) – those areas where homes and wildlands intermingle – understanding wildfire risk is not optional, it's essential. Even if you live in a more urbanized area, smoke from distant fires can significantly impact air quality for weeks on end.

So, what's in the Californian's wildfire preparedness toolkit?

First is **defensible space**. This is the buffer zone you create between your home and the flammable vegetation surrounding it. Cal Fire (the California Department of Forestry and Fire Protection) has specific guidelines, often requiring 100 feet of defensible space around structures. This typically involves:

- Removing dead plants, dry leaves, and overgrown vegetation.

- Keeping grass and weeds mowed short.

- Trimming trees to keep branches away from your roof and chimney.

- Choosing fire-resistant landscaping materials (some plants are much less flammable than others).

- Keeping flammable materials (like woodpiles or propane tanks) away from your home.

Next is **home hardening**. This involves using building materials and construction techniques that make your home more resistant to catching fire from embers or radiant heat. Think:

- Fire-resistant roofing materials (like composition, metal, or tile).

- Covering attic and foundation vents with fine metal mesh to keep embers out.

- Dual-paned windows, with tempered glass on the exterior.

- Non-combustible siding materials.

- Enclosing eaves.

If you're buying or renting in a high fire-hazard area, ask about these features. Building codes in many parts of California now mandate these types_of fire-resistant construction for new homes or major remodels in WUI zones.

Evacuation plans are non-negotiable. Know your local community's evacuation routes. Have a "Go Bag" packed for each member of your household (and pets!) with essentials like medications, copies of important documents, changes of clothes, water, snacks, and a flashlight. Decide on a meeting place outside your immediate area in case your family gets separated. Sign up for emergency alerts from your county and city (often through systems like Nixle or specific county alert programs). Heed evacuation orders immediately. Fire moves fast, and waiting until the last minute can be a fatal mistake.

Be aware of **Red Flag Warnings**. These are issued by the National Weather Service when weather conditions (low humidity, high winds, warm temperatures) are ripe for extreme fire danger. During Red Flag Warnings, be extra cautious. Avoid activities that could spark a fire (like mowing dry grass or using power equipment outdoors).

Air quality during wildfire season can be a serious health concern, even hundreds of miles from the actual flames. Invest in good quality air purifiers for your home. Have a supply of N95 or P100 respirator masks on hand for when you must go outdoors during smoky conditions. Monitor air quality websites like AirNow.gov.

Fire insurance has become a major headache for many Californians in high-risk areas. Premiums have skyrocketed, and some insurance companies have stopped writing new policies or have non-renewed existing ones in certain zip codes. The FAIR Plan is California's insurer of last resort, providing basic fire coverage when you can't get it through the traditional market, but it's often more expensive and offers less coverage. This is a critical factor to research if you're considering buying property in a fire-prone zone.

Again, Cal Fire's website (fire.ca.gov) and your local fire department are your best sources for specific guidance on defensible space, home hardening, and local emergency procedures.

Now for the "other" items in Mother Nature's California welcome basket, often arriving as tag-along guests with their more famous cousins, earthquakes and wildfires.

Droughts are to California what clouds are to Seattle – a pretty consistent feature. The state has a naturally arid to semi-arid climate in many regions, and periodic, sometimes severe, droughts are a fact of life. This means water conservation isn't just a nice idea; it's often a mandated necessity. Expect to see watering restrictions for lawns and gardens, pleas to take shorter showers, and a general societal awareness of H2O as a precious commodity. You might find yourself becoming surprisingly passionate about drought-tolerant landscaping and low-flow toilets.

Where there's fire, there can also be **floods and mudslides**, especially in areas with burn scars. After a wildfire incinerates vegetation, the soil loses its ability to absorb water. Heavy rains, especially those from "atmospheric rivers" (another charming local term for intense storms), can then trigger dangerous flash floods and debris flows in and below these burn areas. If you live downstream or downhill from a recent burn scar, be extremely vigilant during and after heavy rain.

For those lucky enough to live right on California's magnificent coastline, there's the less frequent but still potent threat of **tsunamis**. These giant waves are typically generated by undersea earthquakes, often far away across the Pacific. Coastal communities will have designated tsunami hazard zones and evacuation routes clearly marked. If you feel a very strong earthquake while at the coast, or if you hear official tsunami warnings, head to higher ground immediately. Don't wait for the wave to show up for a selfie.

Then there are the less dramatic but still noteworthy environmental quirks. **"King Tides,"** which are exceptionally high tides that occur a few times a year, can cause minor coastal flooding in low-lying areas, offering a sneak peek into future sea-level rise scenarios. **Santa Ana winds** (in Southern California) and **Diablo winds** (in Northern California) are strong, dry offshore winds that can exacerbate fire danger and sometimes cause power outages due to downed lines or trees. They also have a strange, desiccating effect on everything, including your sinuses and your patience.

This all might sound a bit daunting, like Mother Nature has a particular bone to pick with the Golden State. And sometimes, it feels that way. But the key, as with most things in life, is awareness and preparation. Californians have learned to live with these environmental realities, to respect the power of nature, and to take prudent steps to protect themselves and their property. There's a strong sense of community resilience that emerges during and after these events. Neighbors help neighbors, and communities come together.

It's crucial to remember that while these hazards are real, they don't define daily life for most people most of the time. The sun still shines, the beaches are still beautiful, and the opportunities that drew you here still exist. Being prepared for earthquakes, wildfires, and their various cousins simply means you can enjoy all that California has to offer with a greater sense of security and peace of mind. It's about being a responsible resident of this beautiful, dynamic, and occasionally very lively state.

So, add "earthquake kit supplies" and "defensible space plan" to your moving checklist. Consult those official websites we keep nagging you about. Talk to your new neighbors; they're often a goldmine of practical local knowledge. Embrace the Californian ethos of preparedness. It's just one more way you'll become a true local, ready for whatever the Golden State – in all its shaky, fiery, glorious complexity – decides to throw your way. And who knows, you might even start casually referring to tremors by their Richter scale magnitude at dinner parties.

CHAPTER SIX: Understanding California Speak: From "Hella" to "The Industry"

Alright, so you're getting the lay of the land. You've mentally wrestled with rent that requires a second mortgage on your soul, practiced your freeway merging affirmations, and maybe even scoped out a job that won't immediately plunge you into avocado toast-related debt. Excellent progress. Now, let's tune into another frequency of Californian life: the way people talk. Because, let's be honest, sometimes listening to Californians converse can feel like you've accidentally downloaded the wrong language pack for your brain. It's English, mostly, but with its own unique seasoning, a patois peppered with terms that can leave newcomers scratching their heads, or worse, nodding along cluelessly and accidentally agreeing to something truly weird.

Why dedicate a whole chapter to slang and local lingo? Isn't it enough to just, you know, speak English? Well, yes, you'll survive. But understanding the nuances of California speak isn't just about avoiding blank stares; it's about catching the subtle currents of culture, the inside jokes, the regional pride, and the unspoken rules that float on the sea of conversation. It's about feeling a little less like a tourist and a little more like someone who might, eventually, almost, kind of, fit in. Plus, it's just plain fun to decode a new dialect, especially one that has gifted the world so many memorable, and occasionally mystifying, phrases.

Before we dive in, a crucial disclaimer: California is a massive, incredibly diverse state, and its lingo reflects that. What's common parlance in a San Diego surf shop might sound utterly alien in a Sacramento government office. Slang, by its very nature, is a slippery beast – it evolves, it shifts, it goes in and out of fashion faster than denim trends. What's "hella" cool today might be "hella" dated tomorrow (though "hella" itself has shown surprising resilience, but more on that later). So, consider this a linguistic sampler platter, a collection of common flavors you might encounter, not an exhaustive, Webster's-level dictionary. And as always, your best bet for real-time linguistic fluency is to simply listen.

Let's start with some of the foundational building blocks of Californian casual conversation. First, there's "dude." Oh, "dude." A word so versatile it's practically a linguistic Swiss Army knife. It can be a greeting ("Dude!"), an exclamation of surprise ("Dude!"), a term of endearment ("Aw, dude…"), a mild reprimand ("Seriously, dude?"), or simply a placeholder when you can't remember someone's actual name. It transcends gender, age (to a degree), and social strata. Embrace the "dude." You'll hear it a lot.

Then there's "like." Yes, the infamous, often-mocked filler word. And sure, sometimes it's just that – a verbal pause, a way to gather one's thoughts. But in California, "like" also functions as a quotative ("She was like, 'No way!' and I was like, 'Way!'"), an approximator ("It was, like, ten bucks"), or a hedge ("I'm, like, pretty sure that's right"). Its ubiquity is undeniable. Trying to consciously avoid it might make you sound like a visiting dignitary from a bygone era.

You'll also encounter a constellation of words signifying approval or intensity, many with roots in surf and skate culture. "Awesome" is a perennial favorite, a solid go-to for anything remotely positive. "Rad" (short for radical) still hangs around, often with a slightly retro, yet still acceptable, vibe. "Gnarly" is a classic, capable of describing something incredibly cool or incredibly difficult and unpleasant – context is key. A "gnarly wave" is awesome; a "gnarly wipeout" is definitely not. "Sick" and "ill" can, confusingly, mean "excellent" or "amazing," especially when describing something impressive, like a skateboard trick or a new song. "That beat is sick!" is high praise.

"Cruise" is another versatile verb. It can mean to drive around casually, often with no particular destination ("Let's go cruise PCH"). It can mean to proceed effortlessly ("She just cruised through that exam"). Or it can simply mean to go or hang out

("Wanna cruise over to my place later?"). It generally implies a laid-back, unhurried approach to movement or activity.

If someone is "stoked," they are very excited, enthusiastic, or happy about something. "I'm so stoked for the concert tonight!" Surfers get stoked about good waves, tech workers get stoked about a successful product launch, and you might get stoked when you finally find a decent parking spot. It's a purely positive emotion, a verbal fist pump.

Conversely, a "bummer" is a situation or piece of news that causes disappointment or sadness. "It's a bummer that the beach is closed." It's a concise and widely understood expression of mild to moderate dismay. You might also hear "bummed out" to describe the feeling of being disappointed.

While specific food slang is best saved for our culinary explorations (Chapter 12), you'll notice a general enthusiasm in the way Californians talk about food, especially fresh, local, or trendy ingredients. There's a certain reverence for the perfect avocado, the farmers market haul, or the latest cult taco truck. Listen for the earnestness; it's a tell-tale sign.

Now, let's wade into slightly more contested waters: the subtle, and sometimes not-so-subtle, linguistic divides within the state, particularly the oft-caricatured NorCal vs. SoCal split. The most famous Shibboleth is undoubtedly the word "hella." If you hear someone say "hella," as in "That burrito was hella good" or "There were hella people at the beach," you can be reasonably certain you're in the presence of a Northern Californian, particularly someone from the Bay Area or with roots there. It's an intensifier, meaning "very" or "a lot of." Its usage is a point of fierce regional pride for some, and mild amusement or annoyance for others (mostly Southern Californians).

SoCal, by and large, eschews "hella." What do they use instead for emphasis? A variety of standard intensifiers like "really," "super," or "totally." There isn't one single SoCal equivalent that carries the same regional identity punch as "hella" does for the north. The freeway naming convention, which we touched on in Chapter 2 (referring to freeways as "the 5" or "the 405" in SoCal, versus just "80" or "101" more commonly in NorCal), is another linguistic marker. It's a subtle tell, but one that locals often pick up on. These differences are usually playful, but they do underscore distinct regional identities.

Beyond these general terms, certain industries and subcultures have their own highly specialized lexicons. Perhaps the most pervasive, especially if you find yourself anywhere near Los Angeles, is the language of "The Industry." When a Californian, particularly an Angeleno, refers to "The Industry," they are almost invariably talking about the entertainment business – film, television, music, the whole glittering, soul-crushing shebang. It's spoken with a capital "T" and "I," even if it's not written that way.

If you're in LA, you'll hear Industry-speak whether you work in entertainment or not; it seeps into the general consciousness. Terms like "a general" (a general meeting, an introductory meeting with a studio exec or producer, often with no specific project attached), "on spec" (writing a script or developing a project without being paid upfront, in the hope of selling it later), "coverage" (a written summary and analysis of a screenplay), or "below the line" (referring to the technical crew on a film production, as opposed to "above the line" talent like actors, directors, and producers) are commonplace. Understanding these terms can help you follow conversations that might otherwise sound like coded messages from a very strange planet.

Travel north to Silicon Valley and the Bay Area, and you'll encounter a different, but equally potent, professional jargon: Tech-speak. Here, conversations are peppered with terms like "unicorn" (a privately held startup company valued at over $1 billion), "burn rate" (the rate at which a new company is spending its venture capital to finance overhead before generating positive cash flow from operations), "pivot" (a fundamental change in a company's business strategy, often when the initial plan isn't working out), and "disrupt" (to create a new market and value network that eventually displaces established market-leading firms, products, and alliances). Much like Industry talk in LA, tech jargon often spills out of the office and into cafes, bars, and dinner party conversations throughout the Bay Area.

Given California's extensive coastline and legendary surf breaks, it's no surprise that surf culture has its own rich vocabulary, some of which has already surfed its way into mainstream slang ("gnarly," "stoked"). But you might also hear more specific terms if you hang out near the beach. "Dawn patrol" refers to an early morning surf session to catch the best waves before the crowds or wind pick up. A "grom" or "grommet" is a young surfer. To "kick out" is to properly finish riding a wave by turning back out over the top. Understanding these terms isn't essential for survival, but it might help you appreciate the dedication of those folks in wetsuits.

Similarly, skateboarding, another California-born pastime, has its own lexicon, often overlapping with surf slang but also featuring unique terms related to tricks and terrain. While we won't delve into a glossary of kickflips and ollies here, be aware that these subcultures are vibrant parts of the Californian identity and have definitely enriched its linguistic landscape.

And while we're on the topic of regional specialties, if you find yourself in wine country, like Napa or Sonoma, you'll undoubtedly overhear discussions laced with oenological terms. Phrases like "terroir" (the complete natural environment in which a particular wine is produced, including factors such as the soil, topography, and climate), "legs" (the streaks of wine that run down the side of the glass after swirling, which can indicate alcohol content), or discussions about a particular "vintage" (the year the grapes were harvested) are all part of appreciating California's world-renowned wine scene.

Beyond specific slang words, there are also nuances in pronunciation and common phrasing that can mark you as a newcomer. While there isn't one single "California accent" – the speech patterns in Compton are very different from those in Eureka – you might notice a general tendency towards a more laid-back delivery in casual conversation. "Uptalk," where declarative sentences end with a rising intonation as if asking a question, is sometimes associated with California, particularly among younger speakers, though it's certainly not exclusive to the state.

More practically, knowing how to pronounce local place names correctly can save you some mild embarrassment. Newcomers often stumble over names with Spanish, Native American, or creatively Anglicized origins. For example:

- La Jolla (San Diego area) is "La HOY-a," not "La JOE-la."

- San Rafael (Bay Area) is "San Ra-FELL," not "San RAY-fee-el."

- Sepulveda (Los Angeles) is "Se-PUL-ve-da."

- El Cajon (San Diego area) is "El Ca-HONE."

- Mojave (as in the desert) is "Mo-HA-vee."

- Tuolumne (as in the county and meadows) is "Too-WAH-loo-mee."

- Vallejo (Bay Area) is "Va-LAY-ho."

When in doubt, listen to how locals say it, or discreetly look it up online. No one expects you to get them all right immediately, but making an effort is appreciated.

You might also observe Californians "code-switching," subtly (or not so subtly) adjusting their language depending on their audience. The slang used with close friends at a beach bonfire might be very different from the language used in a professional setting or when talking to their grandma from out of state. This is, of course, true everywhere, but the range of available codes in California can be particularly broad.

Non-verbal cues are part of the communication package too. The "shaka" sign (thumb and pinky finger extended, middle three fingers curled, often with a little wrist wiggle) is a common gesture of greeting, thanks, or general good vibes, especially prevalent in surf and skate culture but understood more broadly. It's like a laid-back "aloha" or "hang loose."

Given the amount of time Californians spend in their cars, it's surprising there isn't more unique slang related to traffic beyond "SigAlert" (which, as we discussed in Chapter 2, is an official CHP term). Perhaps the experience is so universally soul-crushing that it transcends the need for cute nicknames, devolving instead into primal screams and inventive, if unprintable, cursing. However, the shared misery of traffic does lead to a certain type of bonding, where complaining about "the 405" or "the Bay Bridge backup" is a common, almost ritualistic, form of social interaction.

Due to California's rich Hispanic heritage and significant Latino population, especially in Southern California, you'll often hear Spanish words and phrases gracefully integrated into everyday English conversation. This isn't usually slang, but rather a natural linguistic blending. Words like "arroyo" (a dry creek bed), "barrio" (neighborhood), "fiesta" (party or festival), or even a simple "gracias" or "de nada" are commonly understood and used. This Spanglish infusion adds a unique flavor to the local vernacular.

So, how do you, the aspiring Californian, navigate this linguistic landscape? The best advice is simply to listen. Pay attention to how people around you talk – in cafes, at work, in line at the grocery store. You'll start to pick up the rhythm, the common phrases, the local inflections. Don't try to force it by peppering your conversation with every new slang term you hear. Using lingo incorrectly or out of context can make you sound more conspicuous than just speaking your normal English. Authenticity is appreciated.

Remember, too, that slang can be generational. What your teenage neighbor considers "lit" might be completely foreign to their parents, who might still think "rad" is the epitome of cool. And what was cutting-edge lingo a decade ago might now elicit an eye-roll. California has been a linguistic trendsetter for decades, with surf, skate, and Hollywood slang often spreading across the country and even the globe. So, in a way, you might already be familiar with some "California speak" without even realizing its origin.

Some phrases that sound incredibly laid-back can sometimes mask a deeper ambition or a polite way of saying something more direct. "Yeah, no" usually means a definite no. "No, yeah" usually means a definite yes. "Interesting" can be a polite placeholder when someone isn't quite sure what to make of something, or is trying to avoid expressing a negative opinion too bluntly. Deciphering these subtleties is part of the fun.

Ultimately, understanding California speak is less about memorizing a dictionary of terms and more about tuning into the overall vibe. It's about recognizing that the way people use language here often reflects a culture that values innovation, individuality, a certain degree of informality, and a resilient sense of humor in the face of things like earthquakes, eye-watering rents, and soul-crushing traffic.

Don't worry if you don't sound like a local overnight. No one expects you to. Just keep your ears open, don't be afraid to politely ask what something means if you're truly baffled, and enjoy the colorful, ever-evolving tapestry of California English. Before you know it, you might just find yourself saying "dude" without even thinking about it, or maybe, just maybe, you'll even figure out what "no worries" *really* means in any given context. And that, my friend, will be hella awesome.

CHAPTER SEVEN: Picking Your Poison: NorCal vs. SoCal (The Eternal Struggle)

Ah, the age-old question, whispered in hushed tones by prospective Californians and debated with the ferocity of a sports rivalry by seasoned residents: NorCal or SoCal? North or South? Fog or Smog (an oversimplification, but you get the idea)? Welcome, dear mover, to one of the Golden State's most enduring, and often entertaining, internal squabbles. It's a decision that can feel as monumental as choosing a life partner, or at least, choosing which brand of artisanal kombucha truly speaks to your soul. Fear not, for this chapter is your spirit guide through this geographical personality test.

First, let's clear something up: there's no "winner" in the NorCal vs. SoCal showdown. It's not a cage match where one emerges victorious, draped in either a Golden State Warriors jersey or a Lakers one. It's about preference, priorities, and which particular brand of California dream (or manageable compromise) aligns best with your personal operating system. Think of it less as a battle and more as choosing the flavor of your adventure. Both are Californian, through and through, but they offer distinctly different tastes.

Geographically, the dividing line is a subject of much lighthearted debate. For general purposes, think of NorCal as everything from roughly San Luis Obispo County northward, encompassing the San Francisco Bay Area, Sacramento, the majestic Redwoods, and the snowy peaks of the Sierras. SoCal generally stretches south from there, including Los Angeles, San Diego, Orange County, the deserts, and those iconic palm-tree-lined beaches. The Central Coast and Central Valley? They often feel like their own distinct entities, sometimes claimed by both, sometimes proudly independent, like a Switzerland with more agriculture and fewer yodelers. For the sake of this discussion, we'll stick to the broader strokes.

Let's start with the most obvious, and often most fetishized, difference: the weather. SoCal is the poster child for endless sunshine, the land where "winter" often means throwing on a light hoodie in the evening. You can expect warm, dry summers and exceptionally mild winters. Beach days in December? Absolutely plausible. However, SoCal also gifts its residents with "May Gray" and "June Gloom," periods when a persistent marine layer can shroud the coast in clouds until midday, much to the chagrin of sunbathers and anyone who bought sunglasses for practical, rather than purely aesthetic, reasons.

NorCal, on the other hand, offers a more varied meteorological menu. You'll experience more distinct seasons. Summers can be hot and dry inland (think Sacramento or parts of wine country) or famously cool and foggy along the immediate coast, especially in San Francisco where Karl the Fog (yes, the fog has a name and a social media presence) is a beloved, if sometimes clingy, local celebrity. Winters are generally wetter and cooler than in SoCal, with actual snow blanketing the mountains, much to the delight of skiers and snowboarders. Microclimates are a big deal here; you can drive 20 minutes and experience a significant temperature shift. Layering isn't just a fashion choice in NorCal; it's a survival strategy.

Beyond the thermostat, there's the ever-elusive "vibe." SoCal, particularly Los Angeles, often projects an image of laid-back, sun-kissed optimism, mixed with a healthy dose of Hollywood hustle and an undeniable emphasis on appearance and wellness. It's a place where dreams are manufactured, cars are extensions of one's living room, and the pursuit of the perfect beach body is a year-round endeavor. You might find the general atmosphere more overtly casual, with flip-flops being acceptable footwear in a surprising number of situations.

NorCal, especially the Bay Area, often cultivates a reputation for being more intellectually driven, tech-focused, and perhaps a tad more reserved, though no less passionate. There's a strong current of counter-culture history mingling with the relentless innovation of Silicon Valley. You might find conversations lean more towards disruptive technologies or the merits of organic kale than towards the latest celebrity sighting. There's also a deep appreciation for the outdoors, but perhaps with a slightly more rugged, redwood-and-granite flavor than SoCal's beach-centric version.

When it comes to putting food on the table (and affording that table in the first place), the job markets have distinct flavors too, as we touched upon in Chapter Three. SoCal is the undisputed king of entertainment, but also boasts huge aerospace, tourism, international trade (thanks to massive ports), and a thriving biotech scene, particularly in San Diego. The entrepreneurial spirit is strong, whether you're launching a food truck or the next big movie franchise.

NorCal, particularly the Bay Area, is the global mothership for tech. If your resume screams code, data, or venture capital, this is likely your gravitational center. However, NorCal also has a robust biotech sector, is a major financial hub, houses the state capital (Sacramento, with its many government jobs), and, lest we forget, is home to world-renowned wine regions and significant agricultural output. Both regions offer a diverse range of opportunities, but the dominant industries certainly shape the economic landscape and the types of water cooler conversations you'll encounter.

Now, let's talk about the elephant in every Californian room: the cost of living, which we've already established (Chapter One) is roughly equivalent to setting a large pile of money on fire monthly, just for the privilege of existing. Both NorCal and SoCal boast some of the most expensive zip codes in the nation. The Bay Area (NorCal) frequently tops the charts for astronomical housing costs, driven by the tech boom. However, desirable coastal areas in SoCal, like Santa Monica, Beverly Hills, or La Jolla, are certainly not giving away real estate for a song. Generally, your housing dollars might stretch a tiny bit further in some parts of SoCal compared to the immediate Bay Area, but "affordable" is a highly relative term in either place. Inland areas in both regions tend to offer more breathing room for your budget, but often come with longer commutes or a different lifestyle. Chapter Nine will really let you revel in these details.

If the great outdoors is your sanctuary, both NorCal and SoCal roll out the welcome mat, albeit with different welcome gifts. SoCal is synonymous with beaches – miles and miles of them, perfect for surfing, sunbathing, or simply staring wistfully at the Pacific. You also have easy access to deserts like Joshua Tree and Anza-Borrego, and mountain ranges like the San Gabriels and San Bernardinos, offering hiking and, surprisingly, even some skiing, though often on a smaller scale than NorCal.

NorCal's outdoor offerings are, arguably, more dramatic and varied in their majesty. Think the rugged, windswept coastline of Big Sur, the towering ancient redwoods, the iconic granite cliffs of Yosemite Valley, and the alpine wonderland of Lake Tahoe. Skiing and snowboarding are major winter pursuits. The sheer scale and diversity of landscapes, from volcanic Lassen to vineyard-draped valleys, are a huge draw. If your ideal weekend involves serious hiking boots or a kayak, NorCal might be calling your name a little louder.

The general pace of life can also feel different. SoCal, especially LA, is known for its car culture and the traffic that comes with it (as you know from Chapter Two, it's a defining feature). This can paradoxically lead to a life lived in hurried segments between long stretches of gridlock, yet also a certain "mañana" attitude in some quarters. Things might feel more spread out, requiring significant drive times to get from one distinct area to another.

NorCal, particularly San Francisco, is more compact and walkable than LA, with a more robust public transportation system (though still not without its critics or car-dependent suburbs). The tech industry in the Bay Area certainly fosters a high-pressure, deadline-driven environment. However, step outside the major metro areas, and you can find a decidedly slower pace in many of the smaller towns and rural communities. The overall feeling might be a bit more condensed in its urban centers compared to SoCal's sprawl.

Foodies will find paradise in both regions, though with slightly different specialties, as Chapter Twelve will elaborate. SoCal, with its proximity to Mexico, boasts some of the best and most authentic Mexican food you'll find north of the border. LA is a global culinary trendsetter, with an astonishing diversity of international cuisines and a constant stream of new, Instagram-worthy restaurants. Street food, especially taco trucks, is legendary.

NorCal, particularly the Bay Area, is the spiritual home of California cuisine and the farm-to-table movement, emphasizing fresh, local, and seasonal ingredients. San Francisco is a world-class dining destination with a plethora of Michelin-starred restaurants. The access to incredible produce from the Central Valley and artisan cheeses and wines from surrounding regions deeply influences the food culture. Expect a strong emphasis on organic, sustainable, and mindfully sourced options.

When it comess to navigating these sprawling domains, your transportation experience will vary. In SoCal, a car isn't just a convenience; it's practically a necessity for most. The freeway system is vast and complex, and while public transit exists and is expanding, it often doesn't offer the same comprehensive coverage or convenience as having your own wheels. Expect to spend a significant amount of time in your vehicle.

In NorCal, particularly within San Francisco itself, living car-free is more feasible thanks to systems like Muni (buses, streetcars, cable cars) and BART (Bay Area Rapid Transit), which connects the city to the East Bay and other parts of the region. However, venture into the suburbs or more rural areas of NorCal, and a car quickly becomes essential. So, while parts of NorCal offer more transit options, car culture is still very much alive and well across most of the state.

And now, for the part where we tread lightly and with a thick layer of humor: the people. Stereotypes abound, of course, and should be taken with a large grain of sea salt (locally sourced, naturally). SoCal folks are often painted as tan, blonde, fitness-obsessed, and perpetually on their way to an audition or a yoga class. There's the "surfer dude" and the "Hollywood type," both more mythical constructs than everyday realities for most.

NorCal residents, in the popular imagination, might be portrayed as tech-savvy, Patagonia-clad intellectuals who enjoy discussing IPOs and the nuances of third-wave coffee. There's the "tech bro," the "granola-crunching hippie" (a more vintage stereotype, but traces remain), and the discerning wine aficionado. The truth, as always, is that both Northern and Southern California are incredibly diverse melting pots, filled with people from all walks of life, defying easy categorization. You'll find your tribe, whether you're a SoCal sun worshipper or a NorCal fog enthusiast.

The "hella" versus "the" debate (as explored in Chapter Six) is often the most visible, if trivial, manifestation of this regional pride. A Northern Californian's liberal use of "hella" can be a badge of honor, while a Southern Californian's insistence on putting "the" before freeway numbers (e.g., "taking the 405") is an equally ingrained linguistic tic. These little quirks are part of the fun, the secret handshakes of regional identity.

So, how do you choose your poison, or perhaps more optimistically, your paradise? It boils down to what you value most. Are you chasing endless summer, a career in entertainment, and a lifestyle where beach access is paramount? SoCal might be your jam. Do you crave dramatic natural beauty, a more pronounced change of seasons, a tech-centric job market, and a culture that perhaps takes itself a little more seriously (or at least, pretends to)? NorCal could be calling your name.

If possible, spend some time in both regions before making a commitment. What reads one way on paper can feel entirely different when you're actually there, breathing the air (whether it's salt-tinged or eucalyptus-scented) and navigating the daily rhythms. Talk to people who live in the areas you're considering. Ask them what they love, and what drives them crazy.

Ultimately, the NorCal vs. SoCal debate is less about an objective "better" and more about a subjective "better for *you*." Both offer incredible opportunities, stunning beauty, and their own unique sets of quirks and challenges. Both are quintessentially Californian. The eternal struggle is less about which one wins, and more about the delightful agony of having such wonderfully distinct, yet equally compelling, options within one Golden State. Choose wisely, future Californian, and embrace the particular brand of sunshine or fog that speaks to your soul.

CHAPTER EIGHT: Surfing, Hiking, or Just Sitting in Traffic: Choosing Your California Pastime

So, you've navigated the existential dread of finding a dwelling that doesn't require bartering your firstborn, and you've mentally prepared for the vehicular ballet that is the California freeway system. Excellent. Now, for the truly pressing question: what are you going to *do* with yourself in this land of endless (and occasionally interrupted by fog or fire) opportunity? California, you see, isn't just a place to live; it's a place to *do*. There's an unspoken expectation that you'll have a "thing," a pursuit that fills your weekends and possibly a fair chunk of your Instagram feed. And if you haven't consciously chosen one, don't worry, California will happily assign you one by default: the noble art of sitting in traffic.

Yes, let's get that one out of the way. While not a pastime one typically *chooses*, enduring soul-crushing gridlock is a shared Californian experience so profound it practically qualifies for group therapy rates. But true Californians don't just endure traffic; they *optimize* it. This is prime time for devouring podcasts at 1.5x speed, becoming an aficionado of obscure audiobooks, conducting conference calls that make you sound incredibly important (even if you're just debating pizza toppings), or simply practicing your primal scream technique in the soundproofed comfort of your car. Some even claim to have achieved enlightenment somewhere between the 405 and the 101. So, by all means, consider traffic your baseline pastime, the one you can always fall back on. But let's assume you're aiming for something a little more… intentional.

If there's one activity synonymous with the California dream, it's **surfing**. The image of a bronzed figure effortlessly gliding across a cerulean wave is practically on the state flag (it's not, but it feels like it should be). But before you rush out and buy a shrink-wrapped surfboard from a big-box store, understand this: surfing in California is less a casual hobby and more a deeply ingrained culture, bordering on a religion for its devout followers. It's beautiful, exhilarating, and can be incredibly humbling (mostly for your ego, and occasionally your sinuses after an unplanned encounter with a large volume of saltwater).

First, the learning curve. It looks easy from the beach, doesn't it? Just paddle out, pop up, look cool. The reality involves a lot of ungainly flopping, spectacular wipeouts (affectionately known as "getting worked"), and ingesting enough seawater to personally desalinate a small portion of the Pacific. Lessons are highly recommended. Numerous surf schools dot the coast, particularly in Southern California spots like Santa Monica, Huntington Beach ("Surf City USA," naturally), and San Diego. They'll teach you the basics of paddling, popping up, and, crucially, surf etiquette.

Ah, etiquette. This is where many a hopeful surfer runs aground. There are rules in the water, unwritten but fiercely enforced. The cardinal sin is "dropping in" – catching a wave that someone closer to the peak (the breaking part of the wave) already has dibs on. This will earn you, at best, icy glares, and at worst, a stern lecture or an invitation to surf elsewhere, possibly on a different continent. Learn about priority, paddling out wide to avoid surfers on waves, and generally not being a "kook" (a clueless or disrespectful beginner). It's about respect for the ocean and for fellow surfers.

Gear is another consideration. Wetsuits are pretty much standard year-round in most of California, unless you possess the blubbery insulation of a harbor seal. The Pacific is, shall we say, bracing. Boards come in all shapes and sizes, from long, stable foam boards perfect for beginners, to sleek, high-performance shortboards for the experts. Renting is a good way to start before committing to the expense of your own equipment. And remember, that effortlessly cool surfer look often comes with a surprisingly hefty price tag for boards, wetsuits, and artisanal surf wax.

Be aware of the "localism" that can exist at some surf breaks. Certain spots are fiercely guarded by longtime locals who may not roll out the welcome mat for newcomers, especially if those newcomers are perceived as disrespectful or crowding the waves. The best approach is humility, patience, and awareness. Start at more beginner-friendly breaks, observe, and earn your place in the lineup. And no, despite what Hollywood might suggest, shark encounters are exceedingly rare. You're more likely to have a run-in with a grumpy pelican or step on a stingray (learn the "stingray shuffle" – shuffling your feet along the sandy bottom to scare them away).

If the thought of battling waves and territorial locals sounds a bit much, perhaps the call of the trail is more your speed. **Hiking** in California is as diverse as its population. You can find a trail to suit any mood or fitness level, from gentle coastal bluff walks with postcard-perfect ocean views to grueling mountain ascents that will have your quads screaming for mercy.

The sheer variety is staggering. In Southern California, you can explore the surprisingly rugged Santa Monica Mountains, which plunge dramatically into the Pacific, or wander through the otherworldly landscapes of Joshua Tree National Park. Further north, the Bay Area offers iconic hikes across the Golden Gate Bridge, through redwood groves in Muir Woods (pro tip: reserve parking or take a shuttle, it's popular!), or up the slopes of Mount Tamalpais for panoramic views. The Sierra Nevada range, home to giants like Yosemite and Sequoia & Kings Canyon National Parks, is a hiker's paradise, offering everything from easy lakeside strolls to multi-day backpacking expeditions into pristine wilderness. (We'll delve more into avoiding the less cuddly residents of these wild places in Chapter 21, so for now, just picture the scenic bits).

California hiking culture comes with its own set of trappings. Athleisure wear is practically the state uniform for trail-goers. Expect to see a lot of high-performance fabrics, hydration packs that look like they could sustain a small army, and trekking poles even on relatively flat terrain. The ubiquitous Hydro Flask or similar insulated water bottle is a must-have accessory, preferably adorned with stickers from other picturesque locations. And snacks? Forget a simple bag of chips; trail mixes here often resemble a curated selection from a health food store's bulk bin, heavy on the goji berries and artisanal nuts.

The popularity of hiking means that many well-known trails, especially on weekends, can feel less like a solitary communion with nature and more like a slow-moving conga line. Trailhead parking lots often fill up before sunrise. The solution? Go early, go on a weekday, or explore lesser-known trails. There are still plenty of places to find solitude if you're willing to do a little research and perhaps venture further afield. Be aware that many state and national parks require entrance fees or advance reservations, particularly for popular destinations or camping. Always check the official park websites for the latest information on closures, conditions, and any necessary permits.

While surfing and hiking are iconic, perhaps the most universally accessible California pastime is simply embracing **beach culture**, which extends far beyond riding waves. The California beach is a communal living room, a playground, a fitness studio, and a prime people-watching arena. Each beach has its own personality. You'll find an endless parade of activities: intense volleyball games that look like Olympic trials (especially in places like Manhattan Beach or Santa Barbara's East Beach), families building elaborate sandcastles, yoga enthusiasts contorting themselves into improbable poses at sunset, and dedicated sunbathers working on tans that could rival George Hamilton's.

One beloved beach tradition, particularly in SoCal, is the **beach bonfire**. There's something magical about gathering around a crackling fire as the sun dips below the horizon, often with s'mores and a guitar involved. However, bonfires are not a free-for-all. Many popular beaches have designated fire pits, which are often claimed hours in advance, especially on summer weekends. There are strict rules about what you can burn (clean wood only, no trash or pallets), the size of the fire, and when fires must be extinguished. Always check local regulations; fines for illegal fires can be hefty, and nobody wants to be *that* person who sets the beach on fire (in the bad way).

If you prefer your pastimes on two wheels, **cycling** is a major pursuit. California offers a stunning, if sometimes challenging, backdrop for both road cyclists and mountain bikers. Roadies in full Lycra regalia can be seen powering up coastal highways like PCH or tackling grueling mountain climbs. The Tour of California, a professional race, has further cemented the state's cycling cred. Mountain bikers have a vast network of trails to explore, from flowing singletrack through forests to rocky, technical descents in more arid regions. Many cities are also expanding their networks of dedicated bike paths, making cycling for leisure or even commuting a more viable option. Just be prepared for the often-intense devotion to gear and performance metrics that accompanies serious cycling culture.

For those who prefer cooler climes, at least part of the year, **winter sports** are a significant draw, especially for Northern Californians, though SoCal folks make the pilgrimage too. The Sierra Nevada mountains, particularly around Lake Tahoe and Mammoth Lakes, transform into a snowy playground. Skiing and snowboarding are king, with resorts ranging from glamorous, world-class destinations to more laid-back, family-friendly hills. The weekend traffic to and from the ski resorts can be legendary, rivaling the weekday commute in major cities, but for many, the promise of fresh powder is worth the ordeal. There's a certain Californian pride in being able to ski in the morning and, theoretically, be at the beach by late afternoon (a feat more easily accomplished in SoCal, but a fun boast nonetheless).

Beyond these headliners, the list of potential California pastimes is as long as a summer traffic jam on the 5. **Water sports** of all kinds flourish: kayaking and paddleboarding (SUPs are everywhere, from calm bays to open ocean swells), sailing in iconic harbors like San Francisco Bay or Newport Beach, fishing (both freshwater and deep-sea, requiring licenses and adherence to strict regulations), and even outrigger canoeing, reflecting the state's Polynesian connections.

Then there's the unique Southern California spectacle of **grunion running**. Several times a year, on specific nights following high tides after new or full moons, these small, silvery fish come ashore by the thousands to spawn on sandy beaches. It's a peculiar and fascinating natural event, and "grunion greeters" often gather (with a fishing license if they plan to catch any, and only by hand, during open season) to witness this shimmering, wriggling invasion.

Don't underestimate the Californian dedication to **farmers markets** as a serious weekend pursuit. These aren't just places to buy produce; they are social hubs, culinary treasure troves, and a testament to the state's agricultural bounty. Strolling through a bustling market, sampling artisanal cheeses, admiring heirloom tomatoes that look like jewels, and picking up a bouquet of locally grown flowers is a beloved ritual for many. It's a chance to connect with where your food comes from and often, to enjoy some live music and sunshine.

The state's theme parks, from the magical kingdom of **Disneyland** in Anaheim to the movie magic of **Universal Studios Hollywood**, are not just for tourists. Many Californians are devoted annual passholders, navigating the parks with the strategic precision of seasoned generals, knowing all the shortcuts, the best times to hit popular rides, and where to find the tastiest (and most overpriced) snacks. It's a commitment, both financial and emotional, that borders on a lifestyle.

Even seemingly mundane activities can take on a Californian flair. **Dog walking**, for instance, often involves designer doggy outfits, organic treats, and trips to dedicated dog beaches where Fido can frolic off-leash with his equally pampered peers (more on petiquette in Chapter 16). **Stargazing** in the clear, dark skies of California's deserts or mountains can be a profound experience, a reminder of the vastness beyond the city lights.

Whatever pastime you choose, you'll likely notice a certain Californian intensity. People here don't just dabble; they dive in. Gear is often top-of-the-line, even for beginners. Early starts are common, whether it's to catch the best waves, beat the crowds to a trailhead, or snag a prime spot at the farmers market. There's a dedication, an almost professional approach to leisure, that can be both inspiring and slightly intimidating.

The key is to explore and find what genuinely resonates with you. Don't feel pressured to become a hardcore surfer overnight or to scale Mount Whitney your first month here. Start small. Rent gear. Join a Meetup group (a fantastic way to learn new skills and meet people). Take a class. The beauty of California is the sheer abundance of options. Your chosen pastime might be paddling a kayak through a calm harbor, birdwatching in a local marsh, perfecting your sourdough starter (a pandemic pastime that has stuck for many), or simply finding the perfect park bench for reading a book in the sunshine.

And if all else fails, remember there's always the traffic. With the right playlist and a philosophical outlook, even that can become a strangely meditative, uniquely Californian way to pass the time.

CHAPTER NINE: The Cost of Living: It's Not a Myth, It's a Feature

Alright, let's talk about your wallet. Or, more accurately, what's about to happen to its contents once you officially cross into the land of sunshine and, shall we say, enthusiastic pricing. You've already had a taste of the housing market's appetite in Chapter One, and you've pondered how to earn enough to satisfy your avocado toast cravings in Chapter Three. Now, we delve into the glorious, multifaceted, and occasionally breathtaking landscape of California's general cost of living. Spoiler alert: it's not cheap. In fact, consider the high cost of living less of a bug and more of an integrated, non-optional, premium feature of your California experience. It's the velvet rope and the cover charge rolled into one.

Think of it as the "Sunshine Tax," though it applies even when Karl the Fog is giving San Francisco a very personal, day-long hug. This isn't to say you'll be living on ramen noodles cooked over a candle (unless that's your specific aesthetic, in which case, you do you). Millions of perfectly normal people manage to live here without auctioning off their internal organs. But it does mean that your budget will likely need to perform some impressive gymnastic feats, and your understanding of "reasonable" might undergo a significant recalibration.

We've already established that finding a place to hang your hat can feel like a financial extreme sport. But the fun doesn't stop there! Oh no, California has a whole orchestra of expenses waiting to play a symphony on your bank account. Let's start with that four-wheeled appendage most Californians can't live without: your car. While Chapter Twenty will detail the joys of vehicle registration, the day-to-day bleeding starts at the pump. Gasoline prices in California are consistently, and often dramatically, higher than almost anywhere else in the U.S. This is due to a delightful cocktail of state taxes (some of the highest in the nation), environmental fees, and the special "boutique blend" of gasoline required to meet California's stringent air quality standards. Your car might breathe cleaner, but your wallet will be gasping.

Then there's car insurance. In densely populated areas with more cars, more accidents, and higher repair costs (because the mechanic also has to pay California rent), your premiums can easily be steeper than Lombard Street. Shop around, obviously, but brace yourself for figures that might make your current insurer look like a benevolent charity. And should your chariot require servicing, labor rates at garages can also reflect the higher cost of doing business in the Golden State. Let's not forget parking. In major cities, parking can range from "mildly extortionate" for street meters (which are increasingly adept at accepting only digital payments when you only have coins) to "are you kidding me?" for daily rates in downtown garages. You might find yourself developing an eagle eye for the briefly unoccupied curb or becoming a master of public transit Jenga just to avoid feeding the parking meter beast.

Speaking of public transit, while it exists and is actively being expanded in many areas (think BART in the Bay Area, LA Metro, San Diego Trolley), the cost can add up if you rely on it daily. Monthly passes offer some relief, but if you live in a sprawling suburban area, you might find that public transport doesn't quite cover the "last mile" to your destination, or that the time commitment involved makes driving (and its associated costs) the lesser of two evils. And if your commute involves toll roads or bridges, get thee a FasTrak transponder, because those tolls are another recurring character in your financial drama.

Now, let's illuminate the exciting world of utilities, which we touched on when discussing rentals but deserve their own spotlight in your budget. Electricity bills, especially during the sweltering summer months when your air conditioner becomes your best friend, can be a revelation. California often uses a tiered pricing system, meaning the more you use, the more you pay per kilowatt-hour, sometimes at rates that feel designed to encourage monastic living. The state's commitment to renewable energy is admirable, but the infrastructure and development costs can also nudge those rates upwards.

Water, that precious liquid gold, is another utility to watch. With California's perpetual dance with drought, water rates have climbed, and conservation is not just encouraged but often enforced with financial penalties for over-consumption. You'll find yourself becoming intimately familiar with your water meter and developing an almost spiritual connection to low-flow showerheads. Natural gas for heating and cooking, while perhaps less volatile than electricity, still contributes its fair share to your monthly outgoings. And don't forget trash, recycling, and the often-mandatory composting services. While vital for keeping California beautiful (and a topic we'll dive into with gusto in Chapter Ten), these services come with fees that will appear dutifully on your utility bill or property tax statement.

Ah, food. The sustenance of life and, in California, a potential black hole for your disposable income. Groceries here just… cost more. Whether it's the transportation costs to get food to the stores, the higher rents for the grocery stores themselves, or the sheer demand for organic, artisanal, locally-sourced-by-unicorns produce, your supermarket bill might induce a mild state of shock. Yes, the abundance of fresh, beautiful produce at farmers markets is a Californian dream, but it's often a premium experience, not a budget-friendly alternative for your everyday staples.

And then there's dining out. California is a culinary wonderland, from the humblest taco truck slinging divine al pastor to Michelin-starred temples of gastronomy. You could eat out every night for a year and barely scratch the surface. But this delicious exploration comes at a price. That $7 latte you've heard about? It's real, and it has friends. Avocado toast that requires its own line item in your budget? Absolutely. Entrees that cost more than your firstborn's college fund? You'll find those too. Remember to factor in sales tax (which varies by city and county but is generally robust) and a healthy tip, because service industry workers are also wrestling with this cost of living.

We'll give taxes their own dedicated chapter of horrors (Chapter Twenty-Three, you've been warned), but it's worth noting here that California's state income tax is one of the highest in the country, with a progressive structure that takes a larger bite as your income grows. Sales tax, as mentioned, adds a little extra to almost every purchase. And while Proposition 13 limits property tax increases for long-term homeowners, if you do buy a home, the initial assessment will be based on its (likely high) market value, meaning a significant annual bill that also, indirectly, impacts renters as landlords pass on their costs.

For those with little Californians, or plans to acquire them, childcare costs can be genuinely terrifying. Full-time daycare or preschool can rival, and in some cases exceed, in-state college tuition. Nannies? Start saving now. Even after-school programs and extracurricular activities, from soccer leagues to music lessons, can add a hefty sum to the monthly family budget. And while the University of California and California State University systems are world-class public institutions, the cost of in-state tuition, fees, and living expenses for higher education is still a substantial financial undertaking.

Healthcare, which gets its own deep dive in Chapter Seventeen, also contributes to the overall cost of living. Even with insurance, co-pays, deductibles, and out-of-network charges for medical services in California can be significant, reflecting the higher cost of providing care in the state. You'll want to scrutinize your health plan options carefully.

Even the seemingly smaller things, the everyday services, can come with a California price tag. That stylish haircut you're after? Expect to pay more than you might in other states. Gym memberships, especially for trendy boutique fitness classes (a subject for Chapter Twenty-Two), can be a considerable monthly expense. Dry cleaning, pet grooming, home repairs – the labor costs involved in these services are often higher because, well, everyone providing those services also needs to afford to live here.

Let's not forget entertainment and leisure. Those concert tickets to see your favorite band at the Hollywood Bowl or the Greek Theatre? Premium pricing. A day at Disneyland or Universal Studios? A major financial commitment, especially for a family. Even enjoying California's incredible natural beauty, as discussed in Chapter Eight, isn't always free. State and National Park entrance fees, camping reservations, permits for certain trails, and the gear required to comfortably and safely enjoy these pursuits (because Californians do love their gear) all add up.

You might also notice a subtle "California premium" on certain retail goods. It's not always dramatic, but the cumulative effect of slightly higher prices on clothing, electronics, and household items can contribute to that feeling of your money evaporating just a little bit faster than it used to.

Now, it's crucial to reiterate that the cost of living isn't a monolithic entity across the entire state. The financial reality of living in San Francisco or a chic coastal enclave in Orange County is vastly different from that of residing in Bakersfield, Fresno, or a small town in the far northern reaches of the state. As a general rule, coastal metropolitan areas are the most expensive, with costs tending to decrease as you move inland or to more rural areas. However, "less expensive" in California terms might still be "eye-wateringly pricey" compared to many other parts of the country. Do your research on specific cities and regions. Online cost-of-living calculators can be helpful tools for comparison, but always take their figures with a grain of artisanal sea salt and supplement with real-world investigation.

So, how do people manage? Well, as mentioned in Chapter Three, higher salaries in certain sectors and regions help offset some of the costs, but often not entirely. Many Californians become masters of the strategic budget. This might involve embracing the roommate lifestyle well into adulthood (as discussed in Chapter One), becoming connoisseurs of happy hour specials and free museum days, or developing an almost religious devotion to thrift stores and consignment shops. The "gig economy" provides side hustles for many, and a culture of DIY and resourcefulness is common.

You'll learn to appreciate the simple pleasures, like a picnic on the beach instead of a fancy restaurant meal, or a hike in a local park instead of an expensive outing. You'll become adept at spotting a bargain, whether it's on groceries or airline tickets for that much-needed weekend getaway (which we'll cover in Chapter Fifteen). You might find yourself driving a slightly older car than you would elsewhere, or becoming very, very good at making your own coffee.

This chapter isn't meant to scare you off. It's about painting a realistic picture. Forewarned is forearmed, especially when your arm is reaching for your wallet. California offers an incredible lifestyle, unparalleled natural beauty, and boundless opportunities. But these perks come with a significant entry fee and ongoing maintenance costs. Understanding this financial landscape is key to not just surviving, but thriving, in the Golden State. It's about making informed choices, setting realistic expectations, and perhaps, learning to love the taste of tap water (filtered, of course, from your stylish, reusable water bottle). The cost of living here is undeniably a feature, one that shapes the lives of everyone who calls this remarkable, frustrating, and endlessly fascinating state home.

CHAPTER TEN: Recycling, Composting, and Judging Your Neighbors' Bins

Welcome, intrepid mover, to a uniquely Californian arena of self-improvement, civic duty, and occasionally, silent, suburban warfare: the hallowed ground of your trash receptacles. If you thought choosing between NorCal and SoCal was fraught with peril, wait until you're standing bewildered before a triptych of colorful bins, clutching a banana peel and a pizza box, wondering which orifice will accept your offering without incurring the wrath of the Waste Management Gods or, worse, the pitying stare of your enviro-virtuous neighbor. Yes, in California, what you throw away, and how you throw it away, isn't just a chore; it's a statement. It's practically a competitive sport, and your neighbors are definitely keeping score, even if they pretend they're just admiring your drought-tolerant landscaping.

Forget the carefree days of yore when "trash" was a monolithic concept, a single bin filled with the glorious detritus of a life well-lived (or at least, a life that involved a lot of takeout). California, in its infinite wisdom and admirable quest to keep itself from being buried under a mountain of its own refuse, has elevated waste management to an art form, a science, and a subtle test of your moral character. Prepare to become intimately familiar with terms like "contamination," "organics," and the profound existential question of whether that greasy pizza box belongs in recycling, compost, or the general abyss of landfill.

The first thing to understand is that California takes its garbage *seriously*. This isn't just about feeling good; it's driven by ambitious statewide goals to reduce landfill waste, curb greenhouse gas emissions (especially methane from decomposing organic matter), and conserve natural resources. Legislation like Senate Bill 1383, for instance, has set robust targets for organic waste diversion, meaning that slimy lettuce and those coffee grounds are no longer destined for a casual burial. They have a higher calling now. As always, and this is particularly critical in the ever-evolving world of waste regulations, **the specific rules, bin colors, accepted materials, and collection schedules can vary wildly by city, county, and even your specific waste hauler.** Your local municipality's website or your waste management provider's informational pamphlets are your Rosetta Stone. Consult them. Memorize them. Laminate them if you must.

Now, let's meet the stars of the show: your bins. In many, if not most, California jurisdictions, you'll be presented with a trio of wheeled warriors, often color-coded for your sorting pleasure (or confusion). The common lineup is:

1. **The Blue Bin (Recycling):** This is for your "clean" recyclables. Think paper, cardboard, glass bottles and jars, aluminum and tin cans, and certain plastics.

2. **The Green Bin (Organics/Compost):** This is where the real revolution is happening. It's destined for your yard trimmings, food scraps (fruit, vegetables, meat, dairy, bread – yes, even that furry stuff from the back of the fridge), and food-soiled paper products that aren't clean enough for the blue bin.

3. **The Black or Gray Bin (Landfill/Trash):** This is the bin of last resort, the final resting place for items that genuinely cannot be recycled or composted. The goal, in California's ideal world, is for this bin to look perpetually forlorn and underutilized.

Let's dissect the contents of the **Blue Bin** first, because this is where many well-intentioned newcomers stumble. The mantra here is "Clean and Dry." A half-empty jar of peanut butter lobbed into the blue bin is a recycling tragedy. That greasy residue can contaminate an entire batch of otherwise perfectly good paper or cardboard, condemning it to the landfill. So, rinse out those cans, bottles, and food containers. A quick scrape or wipe is often sufficient; they don't need to be sparkling enough to eat off, just free of food gunk. Flatten your cardboard boxes; it saves space and makes life easier for the sorting facilities.

Ah, plastics. The bane of recyclers everywhere. You'll often see numbers (1 through 7) in a chasing arrows symbol on plastic items. For a long time, many of us dutifully sorted by number. However, the reality of plastic recycling is complex and has been in flux globally. Many California municipalities have become more specific about *which* types of plastic containers they actually want in the blue bin, often focusing on bottles, tubs, and jugs, regardless of the number, while eschewing things like plastic bags, film, or polystyrene (Styrofoam), which are notoriously difficult to recycle. **Again, check your local guidelines.** Assuming that all plastics with arrows are recyclable is a rookie mistake. Plastic bags, for example, are a major contaminant; they get tangled in sorting machinery. Many grocery stores have separate take-back programs for clean plastic bags.

Don't forget the **California Redemption Value (CRV),** also known as California Refund Value. This is the nickel or dime you pay on certain beverage containers (beer and soft drink cans, fruit drink and water bottles, wine and spirits cooler containers) when you buy them. You can get this money back by taking your empty, clean CRV containers to a certified recycling center. You'll see folks diligently collecting cans and bottles, and for good reason – it adds up. For many, the convenience of curbside blue bin recycling for these items outweighs the direct financial return, but the CRV system is a cornerstone of California's beverage container recycling efforts.

Now, let's embrace the **Green Bin**, the verdant vessel of virtuous composting. This bin is your ticket to serious eco-cred. Generally, it's for all your "organic" waste. This includes:

- **Yard Trimmings:** Grass clippings, leaves, weeds, small branches, flowers.

- **Food Scraps:** This is the big one. Fruit and vegetable peels, coffee grounds and paper filters, tea bags (staples removed, if possible), eggshells, meat, fish, poultry (bones and all, in many programs), dairy products, bread, pasta, grains. Yes, even the moldy cheese you forgot about.

- **Food-Soiled Paper:** This is a category that often causes confusion. Think uncoated paper products that are contaminated with food and therefore can't go in the blue bin. This includes greasy pizza boxes (tear off any clean cardboard parts for the blue bin, the greasy parts go green), paper napkins and paper towels (if not used with chemical cleaners), paper plates (uncoated), and coffee filters.

A crucial point for the green bin: **NO PLASTIC BAGS.** This is a common contaminant. Even "compostable" or "biodegradable" plastic bags can be problematic for many municipal composting facilities, as they don't break down at the same rate as organic matter or require different processing conditions. Your local program will specify if they allow any type of bag. Many suggest using a reusable pail or container lined with newspaper or a paper bag to collect your kitchen scraps before emptying them directly into the green bin. Some municipalities offer or sell vented kitchen compost pails designed for this purpose. The "ick factor" of food scraps can be a hurdle for some, but keeping a container with a lid in your kitchen (or freezer, for the truly sensitive) can mitigate odors.

Why all this fuss about apple cores and lawn clippings? When organic waste goes to a landfill, it decomposes anaerobically (without oxygen), producing methane, a potent greenhouse gas that contributes significantly to climate change. Composting this material instead allows it to break down aerobically, producing a valuable soil amendment (compost!) and drastically reducing methane emissions. California's statewide push for organics diversion is a big deal for its environmental goals.

Then there's the **Black (or Gray) Bin**, the bin of shame, the repository for what truly cannot be recycled or composted. The goal is to minimize its contents. What goes here? Things like non-recyclable plastics (films, wrappers, polystyrene), broken ceramics or glassware (not bottles/jars), diapers, pet waste (often), and other miscellaneous non-hazardous refuse. If you've done your job with the blue and green bins, this one should be looking pretty lean.

Beyond the "what," there's the "how" and "when." Most neighborhoods have a designated trash day, and a common suburban ritual involves the pre-dawn or late-night wheeling of bins to the curb. There are often rules about how early bins can be placed out and how quickly they must be retrieved after pickup to avoid fines or simply looking like the neighborhood slob. Observe your neighbors. Mimic their bin-related choreography. It's a silent ballet of civic responsibility. Some communities even have rules about which way the bins should face (lids opening towards the street is common, making it easier for automated collection trucks).

Now, let's address the elephant in the cul-de-sac: **judging your neighbors' bins.** Oh, it happens. You'll find yourself taking a casual glance as you walk the dog. Is their blue bin overflowing with pristine, flattened cardboard, or is it a chaotic jumble of wishful recycling and outright contamination? Is their green bin a testament to diligent food scrap collection, or does it look suspiciously empty, hinting at a renegade composter who hasn't embraced the municipal program? This isn't usually overt shaming (though a passive-aggressive note about a rogue plastic bag in an organics bin isn't unheard of in some circles). It's more a subtle, unspoken community standard, a shared understanding that "we're all in this together" to sort our waste correctly. The fear of being the "problem household" with the constantly overflowing black bin is a powerful motivator for many.

This heightened awareness of waste extends beyond your curbside bins. **Reusable shopping bags** are not just a suggestion in many California locales; they're a way of life. Many cities and counties have banned single-use plastic bags at grocery stores and other retail outlets, or charge a mandatory fee for paper bags. Californians have become adept at remembering their reusable totes, often having a collection stashed in their car trunk that could rival a small textile factory. Similarly, the reusable water bottle is an almost ubiquitous accessory, a silent protest against single-use plastic bottles.

You'll also notice an emphasis on **reducing waste at the source**. This might mean buying in bulk, choosing products with minimal packaging, or repairing items instead of immediately replacing them. The "throwaway culture" is definitely frowned upon, at least publicly. This doesn't mean everyone is a perfect minimalist saint, but the consciousness is there.

For items that don't fit neatly into your three bins, California has systems in place, though they require a bit more effort. **Household Hazardous Waste (HHW)**, such as old paint, batteries, pesticides, cleaning products, and fluorescent bulbs, cannot go in any of your curbside bins. These require special disposal at designated HHW collection facilities or periodic drop-off events hosted by your city or county. Improper disposal of HHW can contaminate soil and water, so this is taken very seriously. Similarly, **electronic waste (e-waste)** – old computers, TVs, cell phones – has its own disposal regulations due to the hazardous materials they contain. Many retailers and local governments offer e-waste recycling programs.

Don't forget about **bulky items** – that old mattress, the couch that has seen better decades, the defunct refrigerator. You can't just leave these on the curb whenever you feel like it. Most municipalities offer a certain number of free bulky item pickups per year by appointment, or have designated drop-off locations. Check your local waste hauler's rules before you drag that saggy armchair to the sidewalk.

The sheer variety of local rules cannot be overstated. Bin colors might be different. The list of accepted recyclables or compostables might have slight variations. Some areas might have stricter enforcement or even "trash audits" where dedicated souls might peek into your bins to check for compliance (and leave friendly educational tags if you've strayed from the path). This isn't to make you paranoid, but to reinforce the absolute necessity of consulting your **local, official sources**. Don't assume the rules from your last city, even if it was also in California, apply to your new one.

What happens if you get it wrong? While outright "trash police" kicking down your door is unlikely, repeated or egregious contamination of recycling or organics bins can lead to warnings, fines, or even the refusal of service in some areas. The primary goal of most programs, however, is education and encouragement, not punishment. They *want* you to get it right.

This whole system might seem daunting at first, like learning a complex new dance with three very specific partners. But you'll get the hang of it. Soon, you'll be rinsing out that yogurt container and snipping the plastic window out of that pasta box with the practiced ease of a seasoned Californian. You'll find a strange satisfaction in seeing your landfill bin shrink and your recycling and compost bins flourish. You might even find yourself offering "helpful" advice to a new neighbor who seems to be struggling with the concept of food-soiled paper (try to resist, unless explicitly asked).

Embracing California's waste management ethos is more than just following rules; it's participating in a collective effort to make the state a cleaner, more sustainable place. It's about acknowledging that even seemingly small actions, when multiplied by millions of people, can have a significant impact. So, study your local waste guidelines, set up your kitchen scrap pail, and prepare to engage in the quiet, satisfying, and occasionally judgmental world of California trash. Your banana peels will thank you.

CHAPTER ELEVEN: Dealing with Tourists (Bless Their Hearts)

Alright, future Californian, let's talk about an integral, unavoidable, and occasionally bewildering part of the Golden State's ecosystem: the tourist. They flock here in magnificent, multi-hued droves, drawn by the siren song of Hollywood dreams, sun-drenched beaches, iconic landmarks, and the promise of seeing a Kardashian in the wild (spoiler: less likely than you'd think, unless you're staking out a very specific juice bar). Tourists are the lifeblood of a significant chunk of California's economy, the reason that charming little coastal town has more than one taffy shop, and the source of some truly epic people-watching. They are also, bless their dear, fumbling, map-clutching hearts, sometimes the reason you're late for work, can't find parking within a five-mile radius of your favorite beach, or develop a sudden, intense desire for noise-canceling headphones.

Dealing with tourists isn't about animosity; it's about developing a Zen-like state of acceptance, a strategic approach to navigating your own state, and a healthy sense of humor. Think of them as well-meaning, if occasionally disoriented, migratory birds, sometimes flying in very large, very loud formations, and often leaving a trail of selfie sticks and bewildered expressions in their wake. They are, for the most part, here to experience the same magic that probably drew you to California in the first place, just perhaps with a fanny pack and a more urgent need to photograph every palm tree.

First, it's helpful to recognize the various species of *Touristas Californicus* you might encounter. There's the **Hollywood Hopeful Hunter**, eyes scanning every sidewalk for a celebrity, convinced that every vaguely familiar face is an incognito movie star. You'll often find them congregated around the Walk of Fame, looking slightly disappointed that the stars are on the ground and not, in fact, actual celestial beings. Then there's the **Theme Park Pilgrim**, identifiable by their matching family t-shirts, their meticulously planned ride schedules, and their air of determined fun, even when battling stroller gridlock and thousand-dollar churro cravings. They are a hardy breed, capable of enduring lines that would make a DMV veteran weep.

You might also spot the **National Park Explorer**, often clad in brand-new hiking gear, sometimes underestimating the intensity of a desert sun or the chill of a mountain night. They are on a quest for breathtaking vistas and encounters with nature, though occasionally this involves asking if the bears in Yosemite take credit cards for photo ops. The **Wine Country Wanderer** is another classic, often traveling in packs (sometimes in a slightly wobbly party bus), diligently working their way through tasting menus, and earnestly discussing "notes of oak and despair" after their third vineyard. And let's not forget the **International Visitor**, bravely navigating a new language and customs, sometimes with a delightful literalism (asking where the "Bay of Bridges" is in San Francisco) or a charming bewilderment at American portion sizes.

Now, how do these delightful visitors impact your daily Californian life? Oh, let us count the ways, or at least, the traffic jams. Tourists, with their rental cars often equipped with an overly chatty GPS and a driver unsure if "the 101" is a freeway or a math problem, can add a certain *je ne sais quoi* to your commute. Expect sudden stops in unexpected places, turn signals used as an afterthought (if at all), and a general air of vehicular bewilderment, especially around major attractions. Driving a massive RV down Lombard Street or trying to parallel park a rented muscle car in North Beach? All part of the tourist driving experience, and your subsequent blood pressure spike.

Crowds are another delightful byproduct. That quaint little brunch spot you love? On a Saturday morning in tourist season, it might look like the queue for a Disneyland ride. Your favorite secluded beach? Suddenly discovered by a busload of visitors all attempting to recreate the *Baywatch* opening credits simultaneously. Popular hiking trails can become conga lines of varying fitness levels. Patience, dear resident, becomes your superpower. You'll learn the art of the strategic head-nod as you weave through clusters of people gazing skyward at a perfectly ordinary building, or sidestep groups engrossed in a collective map-reading crisis in the middle of a busy sidewalk.

And the photography. Oh, the relentless, inescapable quest for the perfect vacation photo. Be prepared to become an accidental background character in countless stranger's memories. Tourists will stop, drop, and roll (almost literally) for that perfect angle of the Golden Gate Bridge, the Hollywood sign, or a particularly photogenic seagull. They will pose with statues, with street performers, with unusually large sandwiches. Sidewalks, crosswalks, and scenic overlooks often transform into impromptu photo studios. Your ability to execute a graceful (or at least, non-collision-inducing) swerve will be honed to perfection.

While it's easy to grumble, it's crucial to remember the economic reality: tourism is a massive industry in California. Those fumbling visitors are funding jobs, supporting local businesses, and contributing a hefty sum to state and local tax coffers, which, in theory, helps pay for the services you, the resident, enjoy. So, when you're stuck behind a tour bus doing 15 mph in a 40 mph zone, take a deep breath and whisper, "They're contributing to the GDP, they're contributing to the GDP…" It's a surprisingly effective mantra.

You will inevitably become an unofficial source of information. Lost tourists, like heat-seeking missiles, will lock onto anyone who looks remotely local. Common questions include:

- "How do I get to [impossibly distant landmark] on foot in the next ten minutes?"

- "Where do the movie stars live?" (The correct answer is usually a vague wave towards the Hollywood Hills, followed by a quick escape).

- "Is it always this [sunny/foggy/crowded]?" (Yes. The answer is always yes).

- Various mispronunciations of local landmarks like "La Jolla" (it's La HOY-a, not La JOE-la) or "San Rafael" (San Ra-FELL). A gentle correction is sometimes appreciated; a pained wince, less so.

They might also exhibit behaviors that seem peculiar to locals. Underestimating distances is a classic. California is *big*. Driving from San Francisco to Los Angeles is not a casual afternoon jaunt. Expecting to "do" all of LA's major sights in one day is an act of heroic optimism. Another common sight is attire that is hilariously mismatched to the environment – high heels on a cobblestone street, shorts and a t-shirt in San Francisco in July (Karl the Fog will make them regret that), or insufficient water for a hike in Death Valley. While Chapter Twenty-One will delve into more serious outdoor hazards, simply observing tourist preparedness (or lack thereof) can be a pastime in itself.

So, how does a savvy Californian maintain their sanity and continue to enjoy their magnificent state amidst the throngs? Strategy, my friend, strategy.

Timing is everything. Want to visit that iconic museum or popular beach without feeling like you're in a mosh pit? Go early on a weekday morning. Or try the "local's summer" – in many coastal areas, September and October offer glorious weather with significantly fewer crowds after the school holiday rush. Learning the ebb and flow of tourist seasons in your specific area is key.

Embrace the off-season and discover hidden gems. While the tourists are swarming Yosemite Valley in July, perhaps explore a less famous state park or a different part of the Sierra. Every region has its local favorites that haven't quite made it onto the global tourist circuit. Ask other locals for their recommendations (but maybe not *too* loudly, lest the secret get out).

Develop your "tourist filter." This is a mental skill, honed over time, that allows you to tune out the general hum of tourist activity, the whir of rolling suitcases, the cacophony of different languages. You learn to see *through* the crowds to the underlying beauty of the place. It's like developing selective hearing, but for entire groups of people.

Master the art of giving directions. You will be asked. Often. The best approach is usually friendly, concise, and geared towards someone who may not understand local shortcuts or freeway nomenclature. Pointing is often more effective than complex verbal instructions. Sometimes, a simple, "Oh, that's quite a ways, you might want to use your GPS for that one!" is the kindest response.

Find the humor in it. Honestly, sometimes tourist antics are just plain funny. The sheer determination to get a photo with a costumed character on Hollywood Boulevard, the unbridled joy at seeing a squirrel, the earnest attempts to decipher a Muni map – it can be endearing, in a chaotic sort of way. Laughter is a far better coping mechanism than perpetual grumbling.

Remember your own tourist days. Chances are, before you became a sophisticated Californian resident, you were a tourist somewhere, possibly even in California. You probably asked silly questions, took too many photos, and annoyed some locals. A little empathy goes a long long way. And you will, inevitably, be a tourist yourself when you travel outside the Golden State.

Certain California hotspots have their own unique tourist ecosystems. In **Los Angeles**, Hollywood Boulevard is ground zero, a dazzling, slightly sticky carnival of dreams and celebrity impersonators. Griffith Observatory at sunset can feel like a pilgrimage site for everyone with a smartphone. The beaches of Santa Monica and Venice are a perpetual motion machine of cyclists, skateboarders, street performers, and sun-seekers. Theme parks like Disneyland and Universal Studios are self-contained universes with their own intricate rules of tourist engagement.

San Francisco offers its own set of iconic tourist magnets. The Golden Gate Bridge is a constant draw, with visitors braving wind and fog for that perfect shot. Alcatraz tickets often sell out weeks or months in advance. Fisherman's Wharf, with its barking sea lions at Pier 39 and its sourdough bread bowls, is a sensory overload. And the cable cars? Be prepared for long lines of people eager for that classic San Francisco thrill.

San Diego sees tourists flocking to its beautiful beaches, the historic Gaslamp Quarter, the renowned San Diego Zoo, and the museums of Balboa Park. The vibe is generally laid-back, but the crowds can still be substantial, especially during summer and holiday weekends.

California's magnificent **National Parks** like Yosemite, Joshua Tree, Death Valley, and Sequoia/Kings Canyon are prime destinations. This often means crowded trails, full campgrounds (reservations are essential, often booked far in advance), and visitors who may not be fully prepared for the wildness of these places. You'll see everything from seasoned mountaineers to families attempting challenging hikes in flip-flops.

Wine Country in Napa and Sonoma is a sophisticated adult Disneyland for many. Tasting rooms can get packed, especially on weekends. Large tour groups on buses are a common sight, and navigating the narrow country roads behind a caravan of slightly tipsy sightseers requires patience. Remember that while it's a tourist destination, it's also a working agricultural region.

There will also be moments, dear resident, when you might be mistaken for a tourist in your own town. Perhaps you've paused to admire a familiar landmark with fresh eyes, or you're consulting a map because you're exploring a new neighborhood. Embrace it. It's a good reminder that even locals can find wonder in their everyday surroundings. And sometimes, especially when showing out-of-state visitors around, you'll find yourself adopting tourist behaviors, like taking an excessive number of photos of the Golden Gate Bridge – and there's absolutely nothing wrong with that.

Ultimately, dealing with tourists in California is about perspective. They are a vibrant, if sometimes overwhelming, part of what makes California, California. They bring energy, economic benefits, and a constant reminder that you live in a place that people from all over the world dream of visiting. So, take a deep breath, pack your local knowledge, maybe learn a few key phrases in other languages for bonus points, and navigate the human tides with grace and a smile. Bless their hearts, every single one of them. They're just trying to get a little California sunshine too.

CHAPTER TWELVE: The Perils and Pleasures of California Cuisine (Beyond In-N-Out)

Alright, let's talk sustenance. You've braved the DMV, you've made peace with the rent, and you've even started to understand why some Californians refer to their freeways with the reverence usually reserved for ancient deities. Now, it's time to fuel your California adventure. And while the siren song of In-N-Out Burger, with its not-so-secret menu and devoted acolytes, is indeed a foundational Californian experience (seriously, try it Animal Style at least once), the culinary landscape of the Golden State stretches far, far beyond a double-double and a Neapolitan shake. Prepare your palate, and possibly your wallet, for a journey that's as diverse, innovative, and occasionally perplexing as California itself.

The sheer abundance can be overwhelming. California isn't just a state; it's an agricultural powerhouse, a global crossroads of cultures, and a laboratory for culinary experimentation. This translates to a food scene where "fresh" isn't a buzzword, it's an expectation, and where you can find a Michelin-starred temple of gastronomy a stone's throw from a taco truck serving up life-changing al pastor. The perils? Oh, there are a few. Your bank account might weep, your waistline might expand (affectionately dubbed the "California Stone" by some), and you might occasionally find yourself paralyzed by the sheer number of artisanal pickle options. But the pleasures? They are boundless, delicious, and waiting to be devoured.

Let's start with the official state fruit (it's not, but it should be): the avocado. In California, avocados aren't just an ingredient; they're a religion. They appear in, on, and alongside everything. Avocado toast, that millennial cliché, is elevated to an art form here, often costing more than a sensible pair of socks, but frequently worth every Instagrammable bite. Guacamole is a sacred ritual, and woe betide anyone who suggests adding peas. You'll find avocados sliced onto salads, blended into smoothies, dolloped onto tacos, and even, in some daring culinary quarters, incorporated into desserts. Learning to identify a perfectly ripe avocado by feel is a crucial Californian life skill, second only to parallel parking on a hill.

This obsession with fresh produce is deeply rooted in the state's agricultural bounty. The "farm-to-table" movement, which has become a global trend, has some of its deepest roots right here, with pioneers like Alice Waters of Chez Panisse in Berkeley championing seasonal, locally sourced ingredients decades ago. Farmers markets, as we touched on in Chapter Eight, are not just weekend social events; they are vital conduits between California's fertile fields and its hungry populace. You'll find chefs and home cooks alike poring over heirloom tomatoes with the intensity of jewelers examining precious gems. Seasonality isn't just a suggestion; it dictates menus and inspires culinary creativity. Eating strawberries in December? A true Californian might raise a perfectly sculpted eyebrow.

Now, let's talk about a cornerstone of California's culinary identity: Mexican food. And we're not talking about the gloopy, cheese-drenched facsimiles you might have encountered elsewhere. Thanks to California's history and its vibrant Mexican-American community, you have access to some of the most authentic, regionally diverse Mexican cuisine north of the border. Forget generic "Mexican"; think specific. In San Francisco and parts of NorCal, the Mission burrito – a hefty, foil-wrapped marvel packed with rice, beans, meat, salsa, and often guacamole and sour cream – is an institution. Head south to San Diego, and you'll encounter a different style, with specialties like carne asada fries (exactly what they sound like, and a sublime late-night indulgence) and the fresh, bright flavors of Baja-style fish tacos, often featuring beer-battered white fish, cabbage slaw, and a creamy, tangy sauce. Street tacos are a statewide obsession, with tiny, unassuming taquerias and bustling taco trucks serving up perfectly grilled meats on fresh corn tortillas. Learning your al pastor from your carnitas from your cabeza is a delicious education.

The Asian culinary influence in California is equally profound and delightfully diverse. This isn't just about your standard Americanized Chinese takeout (though you can find that too). In the San Gabriel Valley east of Los Angeles, you'll discover a staggering array of authentic regional Chinese cuisines, from fiery Sichuan to delicate Cantonese dim sum. San Francisco's Chinatown is legendary, but the Bay Area as a whole offers incredible depth in Chinese food. Japanese cuisine also thrives, with sushi and sashimi spots ranging from neighborhood joints to high-end omakase experiences where you entrust your meal entirely to the chef. The ramen boom has hit California hard, with long lines forming for a taste of rich, savory broth and perfectly springy noodles. Izakayas, Japanese-style pubs serving small plates, offer a more casual, convivial dining experience.

Koreatown in Los Angeles is a vibrant, multi-block epicenter of Korean culture and, crucially, Korean BBQ, where you grill your own marinated meats at the table, accompanied by an army of delicious banchan (side dishes). Vietnamese food is another jewel in California's culinary crown, particularly in Orange County's Little Saigon, the largest Vietnamese enclave outside of Vietnam. Here, you'll find soul-satisfying bowls of pho (noodle soup), crispy, savory banh mi sandwiches, and a dazzling array of other Vietnamese specialties. Thai restaurants are ubiquitous, serving up everything from spicy curries to tangy papaya salads. Filipino cuisine is increasingly gaining the widespread recognition it deserves, with its bold flavors and unique dishes. And the vibrant Indian communities across the state mean you're never far from aromatic curries, tandoori delights, and a kaleidoscope of regional Indian specialties.

Given California's extensive coastline, it's no surprise that seafood plays a starring role. From the briny sweetness of freshly shucked oysters (Tomales Bay is famous for them) to the seasonal delight of Dungeness crab in Northern California (often enjoyed simply steamed with drawn butter or in a rich cioppino, San Francisco's signature fish stew), the Pacific's bounty is celebrated. Uni (sea urchin) has a devoted following, its creamy, oceanic flavor a delicacy for the adventurous. You'll find local fish like rockfish, lingcod, and halibut featured on menus, often grilled or pan-seared to let their freshness shine. However, with this abundance comes responsibility. Californians are increasingly aware of seafood sustainability, and resources like the Monterey Bay Aquarium's Seafood Watch program are invaluable guides for making ocean-friendly choices.

All these influences coalesce into what is often vaguely termed "California Cuisine." What does it mean? Generally, it emphasizes fresh, high-quality, seasonal ingredients, often locally sourced. It's usually lighter in style, with a focus on natural flavors. It borrows techniques and ingredients from various global culinary traditions, particularly Mediterranean and Asian, but with a distinctly Californian sensibility. Think grilled fish with a citrus salsa, salads bursting with unusual greens and edible flowers, and wood-fired pizzas topped with artisanal goat cheese and fig jam. It's less a rigid set of rules and more an ethos, an approach to cooking that celebrates the state's bounty and its innovative spirit.

This innovation is also on full display in California's vibrant food truck and street food scene. While taco trucks are the undisputed kings, the mobile culinary landscape has exploded to include gourmet grilled cheese, artisanal ice cream, Korean-Mexican fusion (like the legendary Kogi BBQ tacos), lobster rolls, and pretty much anything else you can imagine served out of a brightly painted vehicle. Following your favorite food trucks on social media to see where they'll be parked next is a modern Californian pastime.

And what do you wash all this down with? Well, Californians take their beverages seriously too. The state's specialty coffee culture is intense. Third-wave coffee shops, with their minimalist decor, single-origin beans, and baristas who discuss extraction methods with the gravity of brain surgeons, are ubiquitous. Expect to encounter pour-overs, AeroPresses, and cold brews that have been steeped for what seems like geological epochs. If tea is more your speed, artisan tea shops offering curated selections of loose-leaf teas from around the world are also gaining popularity.

Of course, we can't talk about California beverages without mentioning wine. While Napa and Sonoma are world-renowned (and a topic we'll revisit in Chapter Fifteen for weekend getaways), California's wine regions extend far beyond these famous valleys. Paso Robles, Santa Barbara County, the Sierra Foothills, and Temecula Valley, among others, produce a stunning array of varietals. Wine isn't just for special occasions here; it's often an integral part of a good meal and everyday life. Alongside wine, the craft beer scene has exploded. California is a mecca for hop-heads, with an astonishing number of breweries producing an endless variety of IPAs (India Pale Ales are practically the state beverage), stouts, sours, and lagers. Brewery tasting rooms are popular weekend hangouts. And let's not forget craft cocktails. Mixology is taken very seriously, with bartenders (or "bar chefs") creating intricate, often expensive, concoctions using artisanal spirits, house-made syrups, and exotic bitters.

California is also exceptionally accommodating to various dietary preferences and restrictions, a true haven for the health-conscious and the culinarily adventurous. Veganism and vegetarianism are mainstream, with dedicated restaurants and extensive options on most menus. Gluten-free is widely understood and catered for. Whether you're paleo, keto, pescatarian, or follow any other specific dietary tribe, you'll likely find your people and your provisions here. Juice bars slinging vibrant concoctions of kale, ginger, and spirulina are as common as Starbucks in some neighborhoods. Health food stores range from large chains to quirky local co-ops, all stocked with organic produce, bulk grains, and every alternative milk imaginable.

Now, for those perils we hinted at. First, the cost. Eating well in California, especially if you're dining out frequently or buying premium organic groceries, can put a significant dent in your budget, as we discussed in Chapter Nine. That beautiful farm-to-table meal or that perfectly crafted cocktail comes with a California price tag. Be prepared for sticker shock, especially in trendier establishments or prime tourist areas.

Then there's the potential for food snobbery or pretentiousness. With such an emphasis on quality, origin, and preparation, conversations about food can sometimes take on an almost religious fervor. You might encounter overly precious descriptions of dishes, intense debates about the best obscure coffee bean, or a slight sense of judgment if you admit you occasionally enjoy a non-organic, mass-produced cookie. Most people are just enthusiastic, but the line can sometimes blur.

Option paralysis is another real danger. Standing before a menu with twenty different types of artisanal tacos or staring at a grocery store aisle with fifty varieties of olive oil can be genuinely overwhelming. Sometimes you just want a simple sandwich, not a lengthy discourse on the heritage of the wheat used in the bread.

And finally, the aforementioned "California Stone." With so much delicious food and drink constantly vying for your attention, and with a culture that often revolves around dining out and culinary exploration, it's remarkably easy to pack on a few extra pounds. Those fresh-baked sourdough loaves, creamy avocados, and decadent burritos are not without their caloric consequences. Moderation, as with all good things, is key, unless your primary California pastime is competitive eating, in which case, carry on.

The true pleasure of California cuisine lies in its sheer, unadulterated variety and the spirit of adventure it encourages. Don't be afraid to try new things. Explore those little neighborhood joints that don't have fancy websites. Ask for recommendations. Sample the offerings at a farmers market. Take a cooking class focused on a cuisine you've never tried. You'll discover hidden gems, develop new favorites, and perhaps even learn to distinguish your Zinfandel from your Cabernet Sauvignon.

Whether you're indulging in a multi-course tasting menu, grabbing a quick and satisfying banh mi, or simply enjoying a perfectly ripe peach on a sunny afternoon, California's culinary scene is an ongoing delight. It's a reflection of the state itself: innovative, diverse, and always offering something new and exciting to discover. So, loosen your belt, grab a fork (or chopsticks, or your hands for that taco), and dive in. Just maybe keep an eye on that avocado budget.

CHAPTER THIRTEEN: Schools, Smog Checks, and Other Bureaucratic Hurdles

Well, hello there, intrepid settler! By now, you've likely wrestled with the Medusa-headed beast that is California housing, danced with the wolves on the freeways, and perhaps even landed a job that allows for the occasional artisanal pickle. You might be feeling rather accomplished, possibly even a little smug. Hold that thought. For we are about to wade into the misty marshlands of Californian bureaucracy, a realm where forms multiply like rabbits, regulations shift like desert sands, and the phrase "some restrictions may apply" is the unofficial state motto. We've already dipped a toe into the DMV (Chapter Four) and previewed the thrill of vehicle registration (Chapter Twenty), but oh, there are so many more hoops to jump through! This chapter is your friendly guide to a few more specific delights: navigating the school system, the sacred ritual of the smog check, and a grab bag of other procedural puzzles designed to keep you on your toes and your printer well-stocked with ink.

Let's begin with a topic near and dear to the hearts (and stress levels) of many a relocating parent: **California schools**. If you're bringing school-aged children, or plan to produce some once you've recovered from the shock of your first mortgage payment, understanding the K-12 landscape is paramount. And like most things in California, it's big, it's diverse, and it can be wonderfully rewarding or maddeningly complex, depending on the day and your local property tax base.

First things first: **public school enrollment**. You'll need to prove residency within a specific school district's boundaries. This usually means brandishing utility bills, lease agreements, or mortgage documents with your California address proudly displayed – the same kind of fun you had assembling your REAL ID package. Immunization records are also a must. California has some of the strictest immunization laws in the country for public and private school entry. While rules around medical exemptions have seen changes, the overarching theme is a strong push for vaccination. **This is an area where laws can and do evolve rapidly, so it is absolutely critical to check the current requirements with the California Department of Public Health and your local school district *before* you show up with your precious offspring and a handful of outdated paperwork.**

California is carved up into a staggering number of school districts, each with its own funding levels, programs, and personalities. The quality of public schools can vary significantly from one district to another, and even between schools within the same district. This isn't unique to California, but the sheer scale and the direct link between local property taxes and school funding in many areas can make these disparities quite pronounced. This, in turn, fuels the time-honored Californian pastime of "school shopping," where prospective parents scrutinize online school rating websites like GreatSchools.org with the intensity of forensic accountants, attend school tours, and sometimes make housing decisions based almost entirely on perceived school quality. It can get competitive, especially in desirable areas where high-achieving schools are a major draw.

Many districts offer **open enrollment** or **inter-district transfer** options, allowing students to apply to attend a school outside of their assigned neighborhood school, provided there's space and certain criteria are met. The availability and process for this vary widely, so you'll need to investigate your local district's policies. **Charter schools**, which are publicly funded but operate independently of some traditional district regulations, are also prevalent in California. They often have specific educational philosophies or focuses and typically admit students via a lottery system if demand exceeds capacity. **Magnet schools**, offering specialized programs to attract a diverse student body, are another option within the public system.

If the public school route isn't your preference, California has a vast array of **private schools**, encompassing religious and secular institutions, various educational philosophies (Montessori, Waldorf, etc.), and a wide range of tuition fees. The application process for private schools can be a journey in itself, often involving entrance exams, interviews, and essays that might make your own college applications look like a walk in the park.

Regardless of whether you go public or private, California does have some state-mandated curriculum. For instance, every fourth grader gets to dive deep into California history, learning about missions, Gold Rush shenanigans, and the various colorful characters who shaped the state. School calendars are generally what you'd expect, though some districts or individual schools might operate on a year-round schedule to accommodate larger student populations. And be prepared for the vibrant, and sometimes demanding, culture of parental involvement. PTAs (Parent Teacher Associations) or similar parent groups can be incredibly active, not just in organizing bake sales, but in significant fundraising efforts that often bridge the gap between state funding and the resources a school desires.

Now, let's clear the air, literally and figuratively, and talk about **smog checks**. If you're bringing a gasoline-powered vehicle to California (that isn't brand spanking new or ancient enough to be a designated antique), you will become intimately familiar with this biennial ritual. Why the fuss? Well, California has a long and storied battle with air pollution, particularly in its densely populated basins like Los Angeles, where geographic and atmospheric conditions create a perfect trap for vehicle emissions. The smog check program is a key weapon in the state's arsenal for cleaner air.

So, what does this ordeal entail? For most vehicles model year 2000 and newer, it's primarily an On-Board Diagnostics (OBD II) test, where a technician plugs into your car's computer to check for fault codes and ensure emission control systems are functioning correctly. Older vehicles might also undergo a tailpipe emissions test. You'll typically need a smog check every two years to renew your vehicle's registration. You'll also need one if you're selling your car, or, crucially for newcomers, when you first register an out-of-state vehicle in California (more on that whole saga in Chapter Twenty).

Are there exemptions? Yes, but they're specific. Brand new gasoline vehicles are usually exempt for their first eight years (though an annual smog abatement fee applies instead). Electric vehicles, naturally, don't need smog checks. Very old vehicles (typically pre-1976 model year, but always verify current rules) are also generally exempt. Hybrid vehicles are typically subject to smog checks. **Again, and we sound like a broken record for a reason, the Bureau of Automotive Repair (BAR) website is your definitive source for current requirements, exemptions, and procedures.**

Finding a licensed smog check station is easy; they're plentiful. Look for the official state sign. Some stations are "Test-Only," meaning they can perform the inspection but can't do repairs if your vehicle fails. "Test-and-Repair" stations can do both. Some are designated "STAR Certified," which means they meet higher performance standards and may be the only stations authorized to inspect certain vehicles (like those identified as "gross polluters" or those directed to a STAR station by the DMV).

What if your beloved chariot fails its exam? Don't panic (much). The technician will provide a report detailing why it failed. You'll then need to get the necessary repairs done by a licensed technician and re-test. If repair costs are prohibitively high, the state's Consumer Assistance Program (CAP) might offer financial assistance for emissions-related repairs to eligible low-income vehicle owners, or even an option to retire a high-polluting vehicle. For particularly tricky cases or disputes, there's even a "smog referee" system. The cost of the smog check itself is usually modest, but if repairs are needed, that's where your wallet can take a hit. Keeping your vehicle well-maintained is your best defense against a failed test.

Beyond the hallowed halls of education and the aromatic bays of the smog check station, California offers a delightful smorgasbord of other bureaucratic hurdles to keep your administrative skills sharp.

Thinking of starting your own business or freelancing (as many Californians do, per Chapter Three)? Get ready for a journey into the exciting world of **business permits and licenses**. Depending on your business type and location, you might need permits from the city, the county, and the state. If you're operating under a name that isn't your own legal surname, you'll likely need to file a Fictitious Business Name Statement (also known as a DBA or "Doing Business As") with your county clerk, which often involves publishing it in a local newspaper for a few weeks. It's a charmingly old-fashioned process in a state otherwise obsessed with digital innovation.

If you become a homeowner (congratulations on scaling that Everest, as per Chapter One!), you may encounter the legendary **California building permit process**. Thinking of remodeling that avocado-green bathroom or building a deck? Hold your horses. Many California jurisdictions have notoriously strict and complex permitting processes for even seemingly minor home improvements. You'll become intimately familiar with your local planning department, zoning codes, and possibly the soothing sound of hold music. Horror stories of projects languishing in "permit purgatory" are a staple of Californian dinner party conversation. Plan ahead, do your research, and consider hiring professionals who are adept at navigating these local labyrinths.

For those in certain professions – doctors, lawyers, nurses, teachers, contractors, architects, barbers, cosmetologists, the list goes on – California has specific **professional licensing boards** with their own sets of requirements, exams, and fees. Even if you're licensed in another state, you'll likely need to go through a California-specific process to obtain licensure here. These requirements can often be more stringent or simply different than what you're used to, so thorough research with the relevant state board is crucial well before you plan to start working.

On a lighter, but still officially mandated note, there's **pet licensing**. Most California cities and counties require dogs (and sometimes cats, though less commonly) over a certain age (usually four to six months) to be licensed. This typically involves providing proof of current rabies vaccination and paying a small annual fee. The license tag on your pet's collar isn't just bling; it's the law, and it can help ensure your furry friend gets back to you if they decide to go on an unannounced neighborhood adventure. Failure to license can result in fines, though it's generally one of the less terrifying bureaucratic encounters.

We briefly mentioned **jury duty** in the introduction, but it bears repeating that as a California resident, you are very likely to receive a summons. It's a civic responsibility, and California courts generally operate on a "one day or one trial" system, meaning if you're not selected for a jury on the day you report, your service is usually considered complete for at least a year. The summons will come with detailed instructions on how to respond, request a postponement, or document an excuse (though valid excuses are fairly limited). Ignoring a jury summons is generally a bad idea and can lead to fines or other penalties.

Finally, be prepared to navigate a fascinating patchwork of **local ordinances**. Beyond the big state and county rules, individual cities have their own sets of regulations that can govern everything from overnight parking restrictions on your street (often surprisingly complex and zealously enforced), to rules about yard maintenance (no, you probably can't let your front lawn return to its native chaparral state, even in a drought), to noise ordinances (that late-night garage band practice might not fly), and increasingly, regulations around short-term rentals (like Airbnb). The best advice? When you move into a new community, spend some time on the official city and county websites. They are treasure troves of information on the myriad little rules that govern daily life.

Tackling these bureaucratic hurdles, whether it's enrolling your child in a school that doesn't require selling a kidney, getting your car to pass its emissions test without divine intervention, or simply figuring out which day to put out the correct trash bin (as discussed in Chapter Ten), requires a certain mindset. Patience, as you may have gathered, is not just a virtue; it's a California survival skill. Cultivate it. Nurture it. Perhaps meditate on it while waiting in a line that seems to have no discernible beginning or end.

The internet will be your closest ally. Most forms, instructions, and contact information can be found online, though navigating the often-byzantine government websites can feel like an archaeological dig. When in doubt, and after you've exhausted your online searching skills, don't be afraid to politely call the relevant agency or office. Sometimes, a human voice can clarify in minutes what hours of web browsing could not. Making appointments, whenever possible, is almost always preferable to just showing up and hoping for the best. And perhaps most importantly, keep meticulous records. Copies of every form, every payment, every piece of correspondence. You'll thank yourself later when some obscure agency questions a transaction from three years prior.

Embrace the forms. Learn their language. Appreciate their subtle variations. You're not just filling out paperwork; you're participating in the grand, intricate, and occasionally baffling tapestry of California governance. And who knows, you might even develop a certain fondness for the heft of a well-completed application, a quiet pride in a successfully navigated bureaucratic maze. Or, more likely, you'll just be really, really glad when it's over and you can get back to enjoying the sunshine.

CHAPTER FOURTEEN: Finding Your Tribe: From Tech Bros to Beach Bums

Well, you've made it. You're in California, or at least you've mentally unpacked your bags and figured out which freeway exit leads to your new abode (give or take a few accidental scenic detours). You might have a roof over your head (even if it costs more than a small European principality), a burgeoning understanding of why avocados are a food group here, and perhaps even a job that doesn't make you weep openly into your organic kale salad. But there's a crucial piece of the puzzle still missing, one that can make the difference between merely existing in California and truly *living* here: finding your people. Your tribe. Your posse. Your fellow weirdos who get your obscure pop culture references or share your inexplicable passion for competitive birdhouse building.

California, in its vast and glorious sprawl, can be a curiously lonely place if you haven't found your niche. It's a land of millions, yet it's easy to feel like a solitary tumbleweed drifting through a very crowded desert. The sheer scale of the place, the car-centric culture in many areas, and the sometimes-frenetic pace of life can make forging deep connections feel like a Herculean task. But fear not, intrepid social explorer! For within this sun-drenched kaleidoscope lies a tribe (or several) for almost every inclination, from the Patagonia-clad tech evangelists of Silicon Valley to the perpetually stoked beach bums of the coast, and every conceivable permutation in between.

The beauty, and sometimes the challenge, of California is its almost infinite variety. This isn't a state where everyone fits neatly into a few pre-ordained social boxes. It's a glorious, messy, vibrant ecosystem of subcultures, interest groups, and lifestyle enclaves, each with its own customs, watering holes, and secret handshakes (or at least, preferred brand of kombucha). Your mission, should you choose to accept it, is to navigate this social smorgasbord and find the folks who make your California experience feel less like a solo expedition and more like a really interesting, if occasionally chaotic, party.

While Chapter Seven already gave you the lowdown on the great NorCal vs. SoCal philosophical divide, it's worth noting how geography often dictates the dominant "tribal" flavors. If you're planted in the fertile crescent of innovation that is Silicon Valley or the burgeoning tech hubs of Silicon Beach (Los Angeles) or San Diego, you will undoubtedly encounter the **Tech Bro** (and his equally driven counterpart, the Tech Sis). Identifiable by their uniform of company-logo hoodies, their unwavering belief in the power of disruption, and their ability to discuss venture capital funding rounds with the passion others reserve for their favorite sports teams, they congregate at industry meetups, hackathons, and co-working spaces that offer artisanal coffee and impossibly fast Wi-Fi. Engaging them often involves nodding knowledgably about the latest programming language or the ethical implications of AI, even if you're still trying to figure out how to work your smart thermostat.

Venture into the glittery heart of Los Angeles, and you'll find the multifaceted tribes of **"The Industry."** As we deciphered in Chapter Six, this refers to the entertainment world in all its glorious, maddening forms. Here, conversations revolve around auditions, pilot season, spec scripts, and who's attached to what project. Networking isn't just a strategy; it's an Olympic sport. You'll find aspiring actors practicing their monologues in coffee shops, screenwriters hunched over laptops fueled by caffeine and desperation, and musicians lugging gear into dimly lit clubs. Entry points include film screenings, Q&A sessions, acting workshops, open mic nights, and any event where there's even a remote possibility of bumping into someone who knows someone.

University towns like Berkeley, Stanford, Davis, Westwood (UCLA), and La Jolla (UCSD) are, naturally, hotbeds for **Academics and Researchers**. Here, the common tongue is often dense with theoretical frameworks and cutting-edge discoveries. Public lectures, campus seminars, and the cozy cafes surrounding these institutions are prime hunting grounds if you enjoy intellectual sparring or simply want to feel a bit smarter by osmosis.

But California's tribes extend far beyond professional affiliations. Many are built around shared passions and lifestyles, and this is where the true diversity of the Golden State shines. For instance, the **Beach Bums and Surf Aficionados**, whose rituals we touched upon in Chapter Eight, form a tight-knit community. This isn't just about riding waves; it's about a shared reverence for the ocean, an almost spiritual connection to the rhythm of the tides, and an encyclopedic knowledge of local surf breaks. Surf shops often serve as unofficial clubhouses, and the pre-dawn gatherings in parking lots overlooking the swells have a quiet, almost religious feel. Environmental activism, particularly around ocean conservation, is often a core tenet of this tribe.

If your heart lies in the mountains rather than the sea, the **Outdoor Enthusiasts** are waiting with open (and probably very fit) arms. Hiking clubs abound, from local chapters of the Sierra Club to more informal groups organizing weekend treks. Climbing gyms are not just places to train; they're social hubs where people swap beta (information about climbing routes) and plan assaults on actual rock faces. Come winter, the ski and snowboard tribe migrates to the mountains, sharing chairlift conversations and tales of epic powder days. These groups often bond over a shared appreciation for California's stunning natural landscapes and a commitment to preserving them.

Then there are the **Fitness Fanatics**. While Chapter Twenty-Two will delve into specific wellness obsessions, the social aspect of California's fitness culture is undeniable. Running clubs pound the pavement in colorful packs, cycling groups conquer coastal highways in tight pelotons, and yoga studios foster serene communities built around shared sun salutations. CrossFit "boxes" (gyms) are known for their intense camaraderie, forged in the crucible of shared suffering through workouts of the day (WODs). Finding a fitness group isn't just about staying in shape; it's about finding accountability partners, cheerleaders, and people who understand your passionate diatribes about the merits of different protein powders.

For those whose passions lean more towards the epicurean, the **Foodie Tribes** are legion. As explored in Chapter Twelve, California is a culinary wonderland, and sharing that appreciation is a popular pastime. Supper clubs, where strangers gather to share home-cooked meals or explore new restaurants, are a great way to meet fellow gourmands. Cooking classes, whether focused on artisanal bread-making or mastering the art of sushi, attract enthusiastic learners. Wine tasting groups delve into the nuances of California's vast viticultural offerings, while craft beer appreciation societies debate the merits of hazy IPAs versus barrel-aged stouts. Even the regulars at your local farmers market can form a sort of tribe, united by their quest for the perfect heirloom tomato.

California has long been a magnet for **Spiritual and Wellness Seekers**, and the tribes dedicated to these pursuits are as diverse as the state itself. Yoga retreats offer immersive experiences in beautiful settings, meditation centers provide havens for quiet contemplation, and New Age communities explore alternative philosophies. You might stumble upon drum circles on the beach at sunset, ecstatic dance gatherings, or workshops focused on everything from crystal healing to mindfulness. If you're on a journey of self-discovery or spiritual exploration, you'll find plenty of fellow travelers here.

The state's strong activist streak means that **Volunteer and Activist Groups** are also a prominent part of the social fabric. Whatever your cause – environmental protection, social justice, animal welfare, political organizing – you can find a group of passionate individuals working to make a difference. Joining such a group is not only a way to contribute to your community but also a powerful way to connect with people who share your core values.

For those who embrace their inner geek, California is a welcoming haven. **Gamers, Nerds, and Pop Culture Aficionados** have ample opportunities to connect. Comic book stores often host game nights or discussion groups. Conventions celebrating everything from anime to science fiction (San Diego Comic-Con being the international mothership, but with numerous smaller events statewide) are massive gatherings of like-minded fans. E-sports are a growing phenomenon, with dedicated viewing parties and local leagues.

And let's not forget the **Car Culture Enthusiasts**. From lowriders cruising Whittier Boulevard to vintage hot rods gathering at local diners, and sleek sports cars congregating at "Cars and Coffee" meetups on weekend mornings, Californians love their automobiles. Numerous clubs cater to specific makes, models, or eras, providing a social outlet for those who find joy in chrome, horsepower, and the smell of gasoline (or, increasingly, the silent hum of a high-performance electric motor).

So, how does one go about infiltrating these diverse tribes? Fortunately, California offers a wealth of resources. **Meetup.com** is practically a Californian institution, a bustling online portal where you can find groups dedicated to almost any interest imaginable, from hiking with dogs to learning Klingon to discussing existential philosophy over craft beer. Eventbrite and similar platforms also list a vast array of local gatherings, workshops, and events.

Don't underestimate the power of **Community Centers and Local Libraries**. They often host clubs, classes, and lectures that can be great starting points. Similarly, **Continuing Education Programs** at local colleges or adult schools offer opportunities to learn a new skill while meeting people who share that interest. **Volunteering**, as mentioned, is a fantastic way to meet people while contributing to a cause you care about. Check with local non-profits or volunteer matching services.

If you're a graduate, your **Alumni Association** might have a local chapter in California that hosts events. And as we'll touch upon more in Chapter Sixteen, **Dog Parks** are veritable social cauldrons for pet owners, where conversations about leash laws and preferred squeaky toys can easily lead to human friendships. If you happen to land in a neighborhood with an active **Neighborhood Association** or a tradition of block parties, consider yourself lucky – these can be instant community builders.

A crucial ingredient in finding your tribe is being **Open and Proactive**. Californians are generally friendly on the surface, but the "California Freeze" is a real phenomenon. People can be busy, schedules can be packed, and it might take more effort to move beyond casual acquaintanceship to genuine friendship. Don't be discouraged if initial attempts don't immediately yield a new best friend. The infamous "California Flake" – where people enthusiastically make plans only to cancel at the last minute – is also something to be aware of. Try not to take it personally; it's often a symptom of overcommitment rather than malice. Persistence and a willingness to be the one to initiate follow-up can pay off.

Online Communities, like local Facebook groups or subreddits, can be a good way to get a feel for a neighborhood, ask questions, or find out about local happenings. While they're not a substitute for in-person interaction, they can be a useful starting point or a way to connect with people who share niche interests, especially in a state as sprawling as California.

It's also vital to remember and celebrate California's incredible **Diversity**. These "tribes" are not, and should not be, homogenous silos. The real magic often happens at the intersections, where different groups and perspectives meet. Seek out opportunities to engage with people from different backgrounds and with different interests than your own. Your experience will be all the richer for it.

Finding your people in a new place always takes time and effort. Don't expect to assemble your dream team of besties overnight. Be patient with yourself and the process. Say yes to invitations, even if they're slightly outside your comfort zone. Strike up conversations in coffee shops, at the grocery store, or while waiting for your perpetually delayed flight out of LAX. Every interaction is a potential connection.

The Golden State, for all its quirks and complexities, has a remarkable capacity to make space for everyone. Whether you're a coding ninja, a surfing shaman, a political firebrand, a quiet lover of books, or someone who just really, really enjoys a good taco, there are others here who share your passions. It might take a bit of searching, a dash of bravery, and perhaps a willingness to navigate a few awkward social encounters, but your tribe is out there, waiting to welcome you to the wonderfully weird and utterly captivating fold that is California.

CHAPTER FIFTEEN: Weekend Getaways: Deserts, Mountains, and Everything In Between

So, you've successfully navigated the labyrinth of California residency, from deciphering your first utility bill (a modern Rosetta Stone) to mastering the art of the polite yet firm freeway merge. You're practically a local. And what do newly minted (or long-suffering) Californians do when the relentless sunshine, the soul-crushing traffic, or the sheer existential weight of avocado prices becomes too much? They escape! Yes, the weekend getaway is a sacred Californian ritual, a vital pressure-release valve, and a fantastic reminder that this state is more than just a collection of bustling cities and eye-watering mortgages. It's a veritable theme park of diverse landscapes, all within a few hours' drive (traffic permitting, of course – a colossal "if").

Forget those anemic "weekend trips" you might have taken in other, less geographically blessed states, where your options were basically "the slightly larger town down the road" or "Aunt Mildred's guest room." In California, you can swap your urban jungle for a Martian desert, trade your surfboard for a snowboard, or exchange your office cubicle for a vineyard vista, all within the span of a Friday-to-Sunday. The sheer variety is staggering, a buffet of environments so diverse it feels like several countries crammed into one state's borders. So, pack your overnight bag (and your patience for the inevitable Friday afternoon freeway exodus), and let's explore some classic California escapes.

Let's start with the **deserts**. When you picture California, you might conjure images of beaches and redwoods, but vast swathes of the state are gloriously, starkly, and sometimes blisteringly hot desert. And they make for surprisingly cool getaways (metaphorically speaking, mostly). **Palm Springs** and its surrounding Coachella Valley resort cities are the reigning monarchs of desert chic. Once the playground of Hollywood royalty, it still oozes mid-century modern cool, with sleek architecture, swanky resorts, an alarming number_of golf courses, and pools shimmering like mirages. You can hike in the nearby Indian Canyons, ride the Palm Springs Aerial Tramway up to cooler mountain climes for stunning views, or simply lounge by a pool with a cocktail, feeling like you've stepped onto the set of a Slim Aarons photograph. It's a place to see and be seen, or to simply bake your stress away under a relentlessly blue sky.

For a more rugged, otherworldly desert experience, **Joshua Tree National Park** is your huckleberry. Its landscape of bizarrely shaped Joshua trees (they're actually yuccas, but don't tell the T-shirt vendors) and massive, jumbled rock formations feels like something Dr. Seuss might have designed after a particularly potent peyote trip. It's a haven for rock climbers, hikers, and anyone who enjoys staring at a night sky so profoundly dark and star-dusted it makes you question your place in the universe. Nearby towns like Pioneertown (an old Western movie set turned quirky tourist attraction) and Yucca Valley offer art galleries, vintage shops, and a distinctively dusty, bohemian vibe. Just remember, it's a desert: bring water, lots of it, and respect the delicate ecosystem.

If extreme is your middle name, then **Death Valley National Park** beckons. As the hottest, driest, and lowest national park, it's not for the faint of heart, especially in summer (when temperatures routinely flirt with "surface of the sun" levels). But its stark, desolate beauty is unparalleled: vast salt flats at Badwater Basin, colorful mineral deposits at Artist's Palette, and towering sand dunes that sing in the wind. It's a place of profound silence and geological drama. Go in the cooler months (late fall through early spring), book lodging well in advance (options within the park are limited), and prepare to be awestruck by nature's capacity for beautiful brutality.

Closer to San Diego, **Anza-Borrego Desert State Park**, California's largest state park, offers a different desert flavor. It's famous for its spectacular wildflower blooms in the spring (if winter rains cooperate), its rugged badlands, and its quirky metal sculptures of prehistoric creatures dotting the landscape. It's a place for solitude, off-road adventures (for those with appropriate vehicles and skills), and discovering hidden oases.

Now, let's ascend from the arid depths to the crisp air of California's majestic **mountains**. If desert heat isn't your cup of tea (or canteen of lukewarm water), the Golden State's numerous mountain ranges offer year-round escapes. **Lake Tahoe**, straddling the California-Nevada border high in the Sierra Nevada, is the jewel in the crown. In winter, it's a world-class ski and snowboard destination, with legendary resorts like Palisades Tahoe (formerly Squaw Valley), Heavenly, and Northstar. The snow is often a delightful "Sierra cement" – heavy and wet, perfect for building a base. Come summer, the impossibly blue lake transforms into a playground for boating, kayaking, paddleboarding, and simply lounging on its (surprisingly chilly) beaches. The North Shore tends to be quieter and more upscale, while the South Shore (with its Nevada-side casinos) offers a more lively, sometimes rowdy, atmosphere.

Further south in the Eastern Sierra, **Mammoth Lakes** is another mecca for mountain lovers. Mammoth Mountain boasts one of the longest ski seasons in North America, sometimes stretching into July. The surrounding area is a paradise for hikers, anglers, and anyone seeking stunning alpine scenery. The dramatic granite peaks, crystal-clear lakes, and vibrant fall colors make it a photographer's dream. It's a bit more remote than Tahoe, which can be part of its charm.

For Southern Californians seeking a quicker mountain fix, **Big Bear Lake** and **Lake Arrowhead** in the San Bernardino Mountains are popular choices. They offer a four-season experience, with skiing and snowboarding at Snow Summit and Bear Mountain in winter, and lake activities, hiking, and mountain biking in the warmer months. These "alpine" villages, with their faux-Swiss architecture and charmingly touristy main streets, provide a convenient escape from the city bustle, though they can get very crowded on weekends and holidays.

No discussion of California mountains would be complete without mentioning **Yosemite National Park**. Its iconic granite cliffs (El Capitan, Half Dome), thundering waterfalls, and giant sequoia groves are globally renowned for a reason. Yosemite Valley is a place of almost spiritual beauty, but also, increasingly, of intense crowds. Planning is essential: lodging and campground reservations often book up months, if not a year, in advance. Entrance reservations are sometimes required even for day use during peak season. Hiking opportunities range from easy valley floor strolls to challenging backcountry expeditions. It's a place that will leave you breathless, both from its beauty and possibly from the effort required to find a parking spot.

For a slightly less frenetic (though still spectacular) giant tree experience, **Sequoia and Kings Canyon National Parks**, south of Yosemite, are home to some of the world's largest trees, including the General Sherman Tree. While they lack a singular, iconic valley like Yosemite, these parks offer vast wilderness areas, dramatic canyons, and a chance to feel truly dwarfed by nature.

And for those seeking a touch of the mystical, **Mount Shasta** in far Northern California looms large, both physically and spiritually. This massive, dormant volcano is considered a sacred site by many, attracting spiritual seekers, climbers, and hikers. The surrounding area offers forests, lakes, and a decidedly off-the-beaten-path vibe.

While we've already dipped our toes in the ocean (Chapter Eight), some coastal areas are quintessential weekend getaway destinations. The drive along **Highway 1 through Big Sur** is legendary, with dramatic cliffs plunging into the turquoise Pacific. It's a place for scenic pull-offs, short hikes to secluded beaches, and a feeling of being on the edge of the continent. Be aware that this stretch of highway is prone to landslides and closures, especially after heavy rains, so always check road conditions before you go.

Santa Barbara, often dubbed "The American Riviera," offers a sophisticated coastal escape with its beautiful Spanish colonial architecture, palm-lined beaches, upscale boutiques, and a burgeoning wine region just over the Santa Ynez Mountains. It's a place for strolling State Street, wine tasting in the "Funk Zone," and enjoying fresh seafood with ocean views. Further north, **Monterey and Carmel-by-the-Sea** provide a charming duo. Monterey boasts the world-class Monterey Bay Aquarium and historic Cannery Row, while Carmel is a storybook village with whimsical architecture, art galleries, and a stunning white-sand beach. The scenic 17-Mile Drive through Pebble Beach is a must-do, if you don't mind the toll. Even further north, the rugged coastline around **Mendocino and Fort Bragg** offers a more tranquil, artsy escape, with quaint Victorian villages, dramatic sea stacks, the quirky Glass Beach, and the historic Skunk Train.

We've also touched upon California's liquid gold in Chapter Twelve, but specific **wine regions** make for delightful, if potentially liver-testing, getaways. **Napa Valley** is the undisputed king, a world-renowned destination for Cabernet Sauvignon and other premium wines, Michelin-starred restaurants, luxurious resorts, and hot air balloon rides over the vineyards. It can be pricey and crowded, especially on weekends. Neighboring **Sonoma County** offers a more laid-back, diverse experience, with a wider range of varietals, a strong agricultural heritage beyond grapes (think artisan cheese and olive oil), and a more sprawling, less concentrated feel. Beyond these giants, consider exploring the burgeoning wine scenes in **Paso Robles** (known for its Rhône varietals and cowboy-chic vibe), the **Santa Ynez Valley** (near Santa Barbara, famously featured in the movie *Sideways*), or **Temecula Valley** (a convenient wine escape for Southern Californians).

Beyond the big categories, California offers some wonderfully unique and quirky getaways. **Catalina Island**, a short ferry ride from the Southern California coast, feels like a step back in time. The main town of Avalon, with its iconic Casino building (which never actually hosted gambling), charming shops, and golf carts as the primary mode of transport, is a delightful escape. The rugged interior of the island offers hiking and wildlife viewing. For a taste of Europe without the jet lag, **Solvang**, in the Santa Ynez Valley, is a meticulously recreated Danish village, complete with windmills, bakeries overflowing with aebleskiver, and shops selling wooden shoes. It's kitschy, charming, and surprisingly convincing.

History buffs will appreciate a visit to **Hearst Castle** in San Simeon, the opulent, eclectic, and utterly over-the-top estate of newspaper magnate William Randolph Hearst. The tours offer a glimpse into a bygone era of staggering wealth and celebrity. Or, delve into California's formative years by exploring the **Gold Country** along Highway 49 in the Sierra foothills. Towns like Sutter Creek, Placerville, and Nevada City retain their Gold Rush-era charm, with historic buildings, antique shops, and tales of fortunes won and lost.

A few practicalities to keep in mind as you plan your California escapes: First, **book ahead**, especially if you're traveling to popular destinations, during peak season, or on holiday weekends. Lodging, popular tours, and even some park entrances can sell out well in advance. Second, **traffic is a travel companion**. Leaving on a Friday afternoon or returning on a Sunday evening can turn a two-hour drive into a four-hour test of your patience and your podcast library. If you can swing it, traveling mid-week or during off-peak hours can make a world of difference.

Third, **California's microclimates are real**. You can start your day in foggy San Francisco and be sweltering in sunny wine country a couple of hours later. The coast can be cool and breezy even when it's hot inland. Mountains have their own unpredictable weather. Layering your clothing is almost always a wise strategy. Fourth, consider investing in a **National Park Pass** ("America the Beautiful" Pass) if you plan to visit multiple national parks within a year, as it can save you significant money on entrance fees. Similarly, a **California State Park Pass** can be worthwhile if you frequent state parks.

Finally, always be aware of **natural conditions and hazards**. Wildfire season is a serious consideration, especially in late summer and fall; check for closures and air quality advisories. In mountainous areas, winter storms can bring road closures and chain requirements. Coastal areas can experience fog or high surf. Being informed and prepared is key to a safe and enjoyable trip.

The beauty of the California weekend getaway is its transformative power. It's a chance to hit the reset button, to explore a completely different facet of this multifaceted state, and to remind yourself why, despite the traffic and the taxes, you chose to make this extraordinary place your home. So, pick a direction, any direction, and go explore. Your next adventure is just a freeway away (give or take a few SigAlerts).

CHAPTER SIXTEEN: Petiquette in the Golden State: Doggie Beaches and Organic Treats

So, you're making the leap to the land of perpetual sunshine and questionable freeway speeds, and you're not coming alone. You've got a furry, feathered, or possibly scaly co-pilot ready to embark on this California adventure with you. Excellent choice! California, by and large, adores its animal companions. From bustling city parks to windswept coastal trails, you'll find a vibrant culture of pet ownership. But hold your organic, gluten-free dog biscuits for a moment. Just as California has its own unique way of doing, well, everything, it also has a distinct code of conduct when it comes to pets. Welcome, dear reader, to the fascinating world of California "Petiquette." It's more than just scooping the poop (though, spoiler alert, that's practically a state religion here); it's about navigating the social and legal landscape with your non-human family member in tow, ensuring you both remain welcome members of the Golden State's grand menagerie.

Before we unleash the hounds of specific advice, remember that golden rule we keep harping on: **local ordinances are king (or queen, or gender-neutral monarch).** What's perfectly acceptable in one sun-drenched SoCal suburb might earn you a citation or at least a very pointed glare in a fog-kissed NorCal enclave. The rules for pets on beaches, in parks, on public transit, and even within your own rented abode can vary dramatically from city to city and county to county. Your new best friends, after your veterinarian and that one neighbor who always has an extra roll of poop bags, will be the websites for your local animal control, parks department, and city government. Consult them. Often.

Now, if you're a renter, you've likely already encountered the first hurdle in the Great California Pet Obstacle Course: finding housing that welcomes your entire entourage. As we lamented in Chapter One, the housing market can be a gladiator sport. Add a pet, especially a larger dog or a breed that landlords have unfairly blacklisted, and you might feel like you're searching for a unicorn that also offers reasonable rent control. Pet deposits are standard, often hefty, and increasingly, "pet rent" – an extra monthly fee just for the privilege of your furry friend shedding on the carpet – is a common feature. Start your housing search early, be brutally honest about your pets upfront, and be prepared to offer a compelling "pet resume" complete with references from previous landlords and perhaps a glamour shot of Fido looking particularly angelic. Some landlords are more flexible than others, but in a tight market, options can be limited.

Once you've secured your (hopefully) pet-friendly Fortress of Solitude, it's time to explore the great outdoors, California style. And this is where the Golden State truly shines for pet owners. Let's talk **dog parks**. They are ubiquitous, ranging from small, dusty patches of fenced-in enthusiasm to sprawling canine amusement parks with separate areas for large and small breeds, agility equipment, and sometimes even water features. Petiquette here is paramount. Your dog should be well-socialized and responsive to your voice commands. Aggressive behavior is a major no-no and can get you swiftly (and rightly) ejected. Always, always, *always* clean up after your dog immediately. Most parks provide bags, but carrying your own is a pro move. Keep an eye on your dog; this isn't the time to catch up on your social media feed. Engage, supervise, and be ready to intervene if play gets too rough. And for the love of all that is holy, if your dog isn't spayed or neutered, check the park's rules – some have restrictions.

Beyond the designated dog park, California offers a veritable buffet of **hiking trails** that welcome canine companions. From coastal bluffs offering whale-watching opportunities for both you and your pooch, to redwood forests where your dog can contemplate the majesty of nature (or just sniff interesting trees), the options are plentiful. However, rules vary wildly. National Parks generally have very restrictive pet policies, often limiting dogs to paved areas, campgrounds, and specific roads, and almost never allowing them on dirt trails (Yosemite and Sequoia, we're looking at you). State Parks are a mixed bag; some are quite dog-friendly on trails, others less so. National Forests often offer more leeway. Local and regional parks are your best bet for finding a wide variety of dog-friendly trails. **Always check the specific park's website before you go.** Leash laws are almost always in effect, and for good reason – you might encounter other hikers, equestrians, or wildlife. Bring plenty of water for your dog, especially on warm days, and be aware of potential hazards like foxtails (nasty grass awns that can embed in paws and ears), rattlesnakes, and ticks. Chapter Twenty-One will give you more on avoiding these less cuddly Californians.

And now, for a quintessential California experience: the **doggie beach!** Yes, there are beaches where your four-legged friend can frolic in the surf, chase seagulls (though hopefully not catch them), and generally live their best doggy life. Famous spots include Huntington Dog Beach in Orange County, Fiesta Island in San Diego, and Baker Beach (certain sections) in San Francisco. However, "dog beach" doesn't always mean "off-leash free-for-all." Many have specific hours for off-leash play, designated off-leash areas, or require dogs to be on leash until they hit the sand. Some beaches that allow dogs might only permit them during the off-season or early morning/late evening hours. Again, **local signage and city ordinances are your guide.** Even if off-leash is permitted, your dog must be under excellent voice control. Not everyone on the beach is a dog lover, and a wet, sandy, overly enthusiastic canine greeting a sunbather who prefers their personal space can quickly turn a pleasant outing sour. And, it bears repeating, scoop that poop. Every single time. Sand dunes are not giant litter boxes.

Speaking of which, let's talk about the holy trinity of California pet ownership: **licensing, leashes, and leaving no trace.** As mentioned in Chapter Thirteen, most California municipalities require dogs to be licensed. This usually involves providing proof of rabies vaccination. The license tag on your dog's collar is your friend; it helps animal control identify your pet if they go on an unscheduled solo adventure. **Leash laws** are the bedrock of urban and suburban petiquette. Unless you are in a clearly designated off-leash area, assume your dog needs to be on a leash, usually no longer than six feet. This is for the safety of your dog, other pets, and other people. Even if your dog is "friendly," not everyone appreciates an unleashed dog approaching them, and not all other dogs are friendly. Retractable leashes, while popular, can be problematic in crowded areas, offering less control.

And then there's the poop. Oh, the poop. Californians are, by and large, militant about picking up after their dogs. You will see dispensers for poop bags in parks, along trails, and even on city streets. There is a profound, unspoken (and sometimes spoken, quite loudly) expectation that you will be a responsible poop-scooper. Failure to do so is not just a social faux pas; it can result in fines and will definitely earn you the silent, burning shame of your fellow citizens. It's a small act, but it makes a huge difference in keeping shared spaces clean and pleasant for everyone. The "pack it in, pack it out" philosophy that applies to wilderness areas extends to your dog's waste in urban settings too.

Now, let's delve into the more... *Californian* aspects of pet ownership. This is a state where pets are often considered full-fledged family members, and the market has responded accordingly. Prepare for an encounter with **California Canine Couture and Cuisine.** Your local pet store might look less like a place to buy basic kibble and more like a Whole Foods for dogs. You'll find organic, grain-free, raw, vegan, insect-based, and bespoke pet food options that might make your own diet look pedestrian. Artisanal dog treats baked with locally sourced ingredients? Of course. CBD-infused calming chews? Naturally.

The pampering doesn't stop at food. **Pet boutiques** offer designer dog collars that cost more than your first car, tiny little hoodies for chilly beach mornings (because Karl the Fog doesn't discriminate), and miniature surfboards for the truly committed canine shredder. **Grooming salons** might offer blueberry facials, pawdicures (with pet-safe polish, of course), and aromatherapy baths. And the services! Dog walkers are a dime a dozen, but you can also find specialized pet sitters, doggy daycare centers with live webcams so you can monitor Fido's playtime from your desk, and even pet massage therapists. The wellness trend has fully embraced the animal kingdom here. Think canine acupuncture, chiropractic adjustments for cats, and even "doga" – yes, yoga with your dog. It's all part of the California package. Embrace the absurdity, or just stick to the basics; no one's forcing you to buy your chihuahua a tiny sombrero, but you'll definitely see it.

This "pets as family" vibe extends to social outings. Many California restaurants with **outdoor patios welcome well-behaved dogs.** It's a delightful perk, allowing you to enjoy a meal or a coffee without leaving your furry companion at home. However, patio petiquette is key. Your dog should be leashed and kept close to your table, ideally lying down. No barking, no begging from neighboring tables (or your own, for that matter), and definitely no dogs on chairs or tables. Water bowls are often provided, but it's always good to bring your own. Remember that health department regulations generally prohibit non-service animals from being *inside* food establishments, so patios are your main dining-out domain.

Traveling within California with your pet can be a joy, thanks to the state's generally pet-friendly attitude. However, if you're relying on **public transit**, rules vary significantly. Some systems, like San Francisco's Muni, allow leashed and muzzled dogs during off-peak hours, while others, like LA Metro, generally only permit small pets in enclosed carriers. Always check the specific transit agency's policy before you try to board with your Great Dane. For **road trips**, California is your oyster. Just remember the cardinal rule: **never, ever leave your pet unattended in a parked car, even for a few minutes.** Temperatures inside a vehicle can skyrocket to deadly levels with frightening speed, even on seemingly mild days. It's illegal, and more importantly, it's incredibly dangerous. Plan for frequent potty breaks, ensure your pet is safely secured in the car, and book pet-friendly accommodations in advance.

While enjoying California's natural beauty, be mindful of **wildlife encounters.** Coyotes are common in many suburban and even urban areas, and small pets can be vulnerable, especially at dawn and dusk. On trails, rattlesnakes are a concern, particularly in warmer months. Keeping your dog on leash and on the trail can help prevent unpleasant surprises. Even in coastal areas, be aware of marine mammals like seals and sea lions; admire them from a distance and keep your dog away to avoid stressing the wildlife or risking injury to your pet. And then there are foxtails, those pesky barbed grass seeds that seem to be everywhere in late spring and summer. They can embed themselves in your dog's paws, ears, nose, and even under their skin, causing pain and infection. Check your dog thoroughly after every outing in grassy areas.

In the unfortunate event that your pet does go missing, having them **microchipped** and wearing a collar with up-to-date ID tags significantly increases the chances of a happy reunion. Familiarize yourself with the location of your **local animal shelters and rescue organizations.** Many California communities have robust shelter systems and a strong network of rescue groups working tirelessly to find homes for animals in need. The "no-kill" movement, which aims to save all healthy and treatable animals entering shelters, has gained significant traction in many parts of the state.

Ultimately, California petiquette boils down to a few core principles: responsibility, respect, and a recognition that you and your pet are part of a larger community. It's about ensuring your pet is a good ambassador for all pets, making it easier for everyone to enjoy the Golden State's many amenities. It's about being mindful of those who may not be as enthusiastic about animals as you are, and taking steps to ensure your pet's presence is a pleasure, not a problem.

So, embrace the organic treats if that's your jam, explore those doggie beaches with gusto, and always, always carry extra poop bags. California can be a veritable paradise for pets and their people, as long as you're willing to learn the local customs and extend a little courtesy. Your furry (or feathery, or scaly) friend will thank you, and so will your new Californian neighbors.

CHAPTER SEVENTEEN: Health Insurance: Because That Urgent Care Bill Will Be Epic

Welcome, brave newcomer, to the chapter that might just save you from needing to sell your newly acquired surfboard (or kidney) to cover an unexpected medical mishap. We're talking about health insurance in California. Now, if the phrase "health insurance" makes you want to immediately lie down in a darkened room with a lavender-scented eye pillow, you're not alone. It's a topic that can induce more anxiety than realizing you've accidentally merged onto the 405 during peak Friday afternoon traffic. But in a state where the sunshine is glorious and the cost of, well, *everything* can be equally dazzling, having a solid health plan isn't just a good idea; it's a financial survival strategy. That "epic urgent care bill" in the chapter title? We're not kidding. A sprained ankle from an overly ambitious hike or a sudden bout of "avocado hand" (yes, it's a thing) can lead to a bill that makes your monthly rent payment look like pocket change.

So, take a deep breath, maybe brew a cup of calming chamomile tea (organic and locally sourced, of course), and let's navigate the thrilling, sometimes bewildering, landscape of California health coverage. Remember, the healthcare world is like the California coastline – constantly shifting. **Rules, plans, and costs can change faster than fashion trends in Venice Beach, so always, always consult official sources like Covered California, the California Department of Managed Health Care (DMHC), and the California Department of Insurance (CDI) for the latest, most accurate information.** Think of this chapter as your friendly, slightly sarcastic GPS, pointing you in the right direction but reminding you to check the real-time traffic conditions.

First off, you should know that California takes health coverage pretty seriously. So seriously, in fact, that it has its own **individual health insurance mandate**. This means that residents are required to have qualifying health insurance coverage throughout the year or face a potential tax penalty when they file their state tax return. This is on top of the federal landscape established by the Affordable Care Act (ACA). California embraced the ACA with the enthusiasm of a surfer catching a perfect wave, establishing **Covered California™**, which is the state's official health insurance marketplace. This is where individuals and families who don't have employer-sponsored coverage can shop for plans and, if eligible, receive financial assistance to help pay for them.

When you start looking at plans, whether through Covered California, an employer, or directly from an insurer, you'll encounter a delightful alphabet soup of acronyms: HMO, PPO, EPO, and sometimes HSA-compatible plans. Let's briefly decode these without making your eyes glaze over.

- **HMO (Health Maintenance Organization):** These plans typically require you to choose a primary care physician (PCP) who coordinates all your care and provides referrals if you need to see a specialist. Out-of-network care is usually not covered, except in true emergencies. HMOs often have lower monthly premiums but can be more restrictive in terms of provider choice. California has some very large, well-established HMOs, like Kaiser Permanente, which operates its own hospitals and medical offices with an integrated care model.

- **PPO (Preferred Provider Organization):** PPOs offer more flexibility. You don't usually need a PCP, and you can see specialists without a referral. You can also go out-of-network, but you'll pay significantly more than if you stay within the plan's preferred network of doctors and hospitals. This flexibility usually comes with higher monthly premiums.

- **EPO (Exclusive Provider Organization):** Think of an EPO as a hybrid. Like an HMO, you typically don't get coverage for out-of-network care (except emergencies). However, like a PPO, you might not need a PCP or

125

referrals to see in-network specialists. Premiums can fall somewhere between HMOs and PPOs.

- **HSA-Compatible Plans (High Deductible Health Plans - HDHPs):** These plans have lower monthly premiums but, as the name suggests, much higher deductibles – the amount you have to pay out-of-pocket before the insurance starts covering most services. They are often paired with a Health Savings Account (HSA), a tax-advantaged account you can use to pay for qualified medical expenses.

The most common way folks get health insurance is still through their **employer**. If you're moving to California for a job that offers benefits, scrutinize the health plan options carefully during your enrollment period. California has its own version of COBRA, called Cal-COBRA, which can provide continuation of group health coverage for a longer period than federal COBRA in some situations, especially for employees of smaller companies. This can be a lifesaver if you find yourself between jobs.

If you're self-employed, a freelancer, or your employer doesn't offer coverage, **Covered California** will likely be your first port of call. You can compare plans side-by-side and see if you qualify for premium assistance (subsidies that lower your monthly cost) or cost-sharing reductions (which lower your out-of-pocket costs like deductibles and co-pays). Eligibility for financial help is based on your household income and size. Open enrollment usually happens in the fall for coverage starting the following year, but if you experience a qualifying life event – like moving to California, losing other coverage, getting married, or having a baby – you can enroll during a special enrollment period. Don't sleep on this; those enrollment windows are firm.

For low-income individuals and families, including children, pregnant women, seniors, and persons with disabilities, **Medi-Cal** is California's Medicaid program. Eligibility is based on income and other factors. Medi-Cal provides comprehensive coverage, often with no or very low monthly premiums. Covered California is the single portal where you can find out if you qualify for Medi-Cal or for subsidies on a private plan.

If you're 65 or older, or have certain disabilities, you'll likely be looking at **Medicare**. This is a federal program, but California has specific options for Medicare Advantage plans and Medicare Supplement Insurance (Medigap) policies that can be purchased from private insurers to help cover costs that Original Medicare doesn't. You'll also find that many California medical groups and hospitals are very experienced in coordinating care for Medicare recipients. It's also possible to purchase **private plans off-exchange**, meaning directly from an insurance company or through a broker, outside of Covered California. However, you won't be eligible for premium subsidies if you go this route.

Now, let's chew on some California-specific gristle. One of the most critical things to understand, especially if you opt for an HMO or EPO, is the **provider network**. California is a huge state, and a plan that has a fantastic network of doctors and hospitals in Los Angeles might have very sparse coverage in rural Humboldt County. Before you sign on the dotted line, rigorously check if your preferred doctors, specialists, and nearby hospitals are actually in the plan's network. This is especially true if you have pre-existing conditions or need ongoing specialized care. Some of California's largest healthcare systems, like Kaiser Permanente, Sutter Health, Dignity Health, Providence, and the University of California (UC) health systems, have vast networks, but their participation can vary significantly from plan to plan. Don't just assume; verify.

On a positive note, California has been a leader in **mental health parity**. State laws often require health plans to provide mental health and substance use disorder benefits that are comparable to physical health coverage. This means access to therapists, psychiatrists, and treatment programs should, in theory, be more robust. However, navigating the system to find in-network mental health providers who are accepting new patients can still be a challenge, so persistence is key. The need for these services is well-recognized, and resources are available, but you might have to advocate for yourself.

Prescription drug coverage is another area that can feel like deciphering ancient hieroglyphics. Each plan has a formulary – a list of covered drugs – often divided into tiers that determine your co-pay. Brand-name drugs on higher tiers will cost you more than generic drugs on lower tiers. Some plans may require prior authorization for certain medications or have step therapy protocols (meaning you have to try a less expensive drug before they'll cover a more expensive one). If you take regular medications, check the plan's formulary carefully before enrolling.

A uniquely Californian lifesaver you should know about is the state's protection against **surprise medical bills**, sometimes called balance billing. If you have state-regulated health insurance and receive emergency care at an out-of-network hospital, or non-emergency care from an out-of-network provider at an in-network facility (like an anesthesiologist you didn't choose), California law (Assembly Bill 72, for example) helps protect you from being billed for the difference between what the provider charges and what your insurance pays. This doesn't cover all situations, and rules apply, but it's a significant consumer protection that can prevent those heart-stopping, unexpected bills that can run into tens or even hundreds of thousands of dollars. The DMHC and CDI websites have detailed information on these protections.

Let's be brutally honest: even with insurance, healthcare in California can be expensive. The overall cost of providing medical care in the state is high, and this is reflected in premiums, deductibles, co-pays, and co-insurance. That "affordable" plan on Covered California might still come with a $6,000 individual deductible. This means you could be paying quite a bit out-of-pocket before your insurance coverage really kicks in for non-preventive services. Factor these potential out-of-pocket maximums into your overall budget. Preventive care, however, such as annual check-ups, flu shots, and certain screenings, is generally covered at no cost to you under ACA-compliant plans. Take advantage of these!

So, how do you wade through this without losing your mind or your life savings?

First, **do your homework obsessively.** Don't just pick the plan with the lowest premium. Look at the deductible, the out-of-pocket maximum, the co-pays for doctor visits and prescriptions, and, crucially, the provider network. Think about your typical healthcare usage. Are you generally healthy, or do you have chronic conditions requiring frequent specialist visits?

Second, **utilize the available resources.** Covered California has certified enrollers and insurance agents who can provide free, personalized assistance with choosing a plan. The DMHC (for HMOs and some PPOs) and the CDI (for most PPOs and other types of coverage) are state agencies that regulate health plans and can help if you have a problem with your insurer. They also have helplines and extensive consumer information on their websites.

Third, **understand your plan once you have it.** Read that Evidence of Coverage booklet, even if it looks like it could tranquillize a rhino. Know how to get referrals, what the emergency care protocols are, and how to file a grievance if necessary.

Fourth, **be your own advocate.** Don't be afraid to ask questions – of your doctor, your insurer, your HR department. If a bill looks wrong, challenge it. If you're denied coverage for something you believe should be covered, appeal it. The system can be complex, but you have rights.

Choosing a health plan is one of an adultier adult's least favorite tasks, right up there with assembling flat-pack furniture or listening to a timeshare presentation. But in California, it's a non-negotiable part of setting yourself up for success and peace of mind. A little bit of research and careful planning on the front end can save you a world of financial pain and logistical headaches down the road. Because while the California dream often involves sunshine and scenic vistas, it definitely doesn't include being bankrupted by a rogue gallbladder or an ill-advised attempt to learn how to skateboard at age forty-something. Get covered. Your future self (and your bank account) will thank you profusely.

CHAPTER EIGHTEEN: Utilities and Other Essential Adulting in California

Alright, you've made it this far. You've battled for housing, tamed (sort of) the freeways, and maybe even figured out which end of a surfboard goes forward. Congratulations! You're practically a seasoned Californian. Except, now you have to do the *really* glamorous stuff: keeping the lights on, the water flowing, and the Wi-Fi signal strong enough to stream your existential dread away. Welcome, friend, to the wonderful world of California utilities and other essential "adulting" tasks that will make you yearn for the simple days of just figuring out which bin takes the greasy pizza box. Fear not, this isn't rocket science, but it does have its own distinctly Californian flavor, often involving more paperwork than a peace treaty and a deeper understanding of acronyms than a government agent.

First up, let's talk about keeping your humble abode illuminated and your showers something other than bracingly Arctic: **electricity and natural gas**. For many Californians, their energy overlords will be one of a few major players. In Northern California, **Pacific Gas and Electric (PG&E)** is the dominant force, a company so woven into the fabric of the state it practically has its own zip code. Southern Californians are often served by **Southern California Edison (SCE)** for electricity and **SoCalGas** for natural gas. San Diego and parts of southern Orange County usually fall under the purview of **San Diego Gas & Electric (SDG&E)**. There are also numerous municipal utility districts, like the **Los Angeles Department of Water and Power (LADWP)** or the **Sacramento Municipal Utility District (SMUD)**, which handle electricity (and sometimes water) for their respective city residents, often with their own unique rules and rate structures.

Setting up service usually involves an online application or a phone call. You'll need your new address, some form of identification, and possibly a deposit if your credit history isn't as sparkling as a freshly detailed Tesla. Be prepared to provide the date you want service to start, and don't leave it to the last minute, especially if you're moving into a place that's been vacant, as it might require a technician to visit. Once service is established, you'll enter the exciting realm of the California utility bill. These documents can be masterpieces of complexity, often featuring tiered rates for electricity (the more you use, the higher the rate per kilowatt-hour climbs), various taxes and surcharges funding things like energy efficiency programs and assistance for low-income customers (often bundled under "Public Purpose Programs"), and sometimes, a separate charge for "transmission" and "distribution." It's like a tasting menu where every course costs money you didn't realize you'd ordered.

A growing feature in California's energy landscape is **Community Choice Aggregation (CCA)**, also known as Community Choice Energy (CCE). In many areas, you might find your electricity generation is handled by a local CCA, while the traditional utility (like PG&E or SCE) still manages the transmission, distribution, billing, and power lines. CCAs aim to provide residents and businesses with more choice, often with an emphasis on sourcing a higher percentage of electricity from renewable sources like solar and wind. You're typically automatically enrolled if a CCA serves your area, but you usually have the option to opt out and stick with the traditional utility's generation mix. Your bill will still come from the utility, but it will show charges for the CCA's generation services. It's all part of California's ambitious push towards a cleaner energy future, and a delightful extra layer of complexity for you to decipher.

Next, let's turn on the taps with **water and wastewater (sewer) services**. Unlike electricity and gas, your water provider is almost always determined by your geographical location and is typically a municipal agency, a special water district, or a publicly regulated private water company. Finding out who serves your address might require a quick search on your city or county website. Setting up service is similar to other utilities – an application, ID, and possibly a deposit. California water bills can also have their own quirks. You'll likely see charges for the amount of water consumed, a fixed service charge, and potentially surcharges related to drought conditions, water conservation programs, or infrastructure improvements.

Given California's often-parched conditions, water conservation is not just a suggestion; it's a way of life, and it's increasingly reflected in your utility interactions. Many water agencies have tiered rates designed to penalize excessive water use. You might also encounter information about rebates for installing water-efficient appliances (like toilets and washing machines) or for converting thirsty lawns to drought-tolerant landscaping. Pay attention to local watering restrictions, especially during declared droughts; violations can lead to warnings or fines. Understanding your water bill isn't just about budgeting; it's about being a responsible H2O citizen in a state that frequently wishes it had more of it. Wastewater or sewer charges are often bundled with your water bill or may come as a separate bill from your city or a sanitation district, usually based on water usage or a flat fee.

Now, for the stuff you want to get rid of: **trash, recycling, and organics collection**. As we celebrated with much fanfare in Chapter Ten, California is serious about sorting its waste. Your city or county will have an exclusive agreement with a specific waste hauling company, or the municipality itself may provide the service. You generally don't get to choose your provider. When you set up your other utilities like water, you're often automatically enrolled for trash service, or you may need to contact the designated hauler directly. The cost for these services will typically appear on a combined utility bill from your city, as a separate bill from the hauler, or sometimes even on your property tax bill.

You'll receive those color-coded bins (blue for recycling, green for organics/compost, black/gray for landfill), along with a collection schedule and a detailed list of what goes where. Fees can vary based on the size of your landfill bin (smaller landfill bins often mean lower charges, incentivizing you to recycle and compost more), and there might be extra charges for oversized items or additional pickups. Remember, contamination is the enemy. A plastic bag in the green bin or food waste in the blue bin can cause problems for the entire system. Familiarize yourself with your local rules – they are gospel.

Let's get connected with **internet, cable, and phone services**. In the land of Silicon Valley, you'd expect lightning-fast, universally available internet, right? Well, sometimes. Major providers like Xfinity (Comcast), Spectrum (Charter), AT&T, and Frontier are widely available, offering various bundles of internet, cable TV, and sometimes phone service. However, depending on your exact location, especially in more rural areas or even some surprisingly underserved urban pockets, your choices might be limited, and the promised speeds might be more "dial-up nostalgia" than "fiber optic dream." Do your research on which providers serve your specific address. Websites like BroadbandNow can be helpful starting points, but always confirm directly with the providers.

Setting up new service often involves choosing a plan (deciphering promotional rates versus what you'll pay after the first year is a fun game), scheduling an installation (the infamous four-hour arrival window is alive and well), and possibly paying an installation fee or equipment rental charges. If you're a cord-cutter, standalone internet will be your focus, and you'll find a robust market for streaming services to fill your entertainment needs. Fiber optic service, offering the fastest speeds, is expanding but isn't available everywhere. Be prepared for the occasional outage and the unique joy of troubleshooting with customer service. If you're moving into an apartment complex, sometimes the building has an exclusive agreement with one provider, limiting your choices.

Beyond these core utilities, there are a few other "adulting" nuts and bolts to tighten down as you settle into California. While Chapter Seventeen covered the critical importance of health insurance, and Chapter Five touched upon earthquake insurance as a concept, the actual process of **obtaining renters or homeowners insurance** is a key step. Standard policies cover things like fire, theft, and liability, but as mentioned, earthquake coverage is almost always a separate policy or endorsement, and flood insurance (if you're in a flood zone) is also separate. Given

California's propensity for seismic shimmies and occasional deluges, carefully evaluating your need for these additional coverages is a prudent adulting move. Shop around, as rates can vary.

Pest control is another delightful aspect of California living that might require some adult-level decision-making. Depending on your location and the type of dwelling, you might encounter unwelcome guests like ants (a California staple), spiders (including black widows and brown recluses in some areas), termites (especially in older wooden structures), or rodents. Many Californians opt for regular preventative pest control services, either through a contract with a professional company or by diligently applying DIY treatments. If you're renting, your lease should specify who is responsible for pest control, but it's often a shared responsibility or falls to the landlord for structural issues like termites. Understanding what's skittering in your walls is part of the California charm.

If you've moved into a home with a yard, particularly one with that quintessential California lawn you're now feeling guilty about watering, **landscaping and garden maintenance** becomes an ongoing task. You can either embrace your inner green thumb or hire a gardening service, which are plentiful. Given water restrictions, many are shifting to drought-tolerant plants, succulents, and hardscaping, which might involve an initial investment but can save water and maintenance in the long run. Your city or water district might even offer rebates for lawn removal.

Finally, a small but crucial detail: ensuring your **mailing address is correctly updated** with everyone who matters – banks, credit card companies, subscription services, your Aunt Mildred who still sends fruitcakes. While the USPS mail forwarding service is your first line of defense, diligently updating your address directly with important entities will prevent your sensitive documents from embarking on their own California adventure without you. And if you're living in an apartment complex with a communal mailroom, get to know your mail carrier; they are unsung heroes.

Setting up and managing utilities and these other essential adulting tasks in California isn't always a walk on a sun-kissed beach. It requires diligence, patience, and a willingness to navigate systems that can sometimes feel designed by a committee that only communicates via carrier pigeon. But with a bit of preparation and a healthy sense of humor, you'll have the lights on, the water flowing, the Wi-Fi humming, and your little corner of the Golden State running smoothly. Now, if you could just figure out where you put that welcome packet with the trash pickup schedule...

CHAPTER NINETEEN: The California Dream vs. The California Reality: Managing Expectations

Ah, the California Dream. It shimmers on the horizon of the American consciousness like a heat haze on the Mojave, a potent cocktail of endless sunshine, boundless opportunity, and the vague promise that you, too, can become a slightly more tan, significantly more relaxed version of your current self, possibly while learning to surf or accidentally inventing the next world-changing app. It's been bottled, sold, and sung about for generations, a siren song luring hopefuls westward with visions of golden beaches, Hollywood stardom, and a life where "making it" seems as inevitable as a perfect sunset over the Pacific. If you're reading this chapter, chances are a sliver of that dream has taken root in your imagination, watered by movies, music, and those infuriatingly perfect Instagram feeds.

Now, we're not here to stomp on your aspirations with the steel-toed boot of cynicism. That dream, in its myriad forms, is a powerful motivator and a beautiful thing. But this is the chapter where we gently, humorously, and with a healthy dose of realism, adjust the focus a little. Think of it as cleaning the smudges off the rose-tinted glasses before you sign that eye-wateringly expensive lease. Because the California Dream, like any dream, can look a bit different when the alarm clock of reality goes off. It's not about shattering the dream, but about understanding its real-world operating system so you can navigate it without too many bewildering system crashes.

One of the first things you'll encounter is the concept of the "Sunshine Tax," a term locals use with a knowing sigh. It's the unspoken premium you pay for the generally delightful weather and the lifestyle that comes with it. This isn't a literal tax (though, as you'll discover in Chapter Twenty-Three, there are plenty of those too), but rather the inflated cost of almost everything, from that charming bungalow you envisioned (which turns out to be a "cozy" shed in someone's backyard, as per Chapter One) to the price of a single, locally sourced, organically grown peach. The dream of easy, sun-drenched living often collides with the reality that maintaining that dream requires a significant and steady flow of a different kind of green.

The dream of California often includes a vision of boundless economic opportunity, a place where fortunes are made and careers take flight. And yes, as we touched on in Chapter Three, California boasts an enormous and dynamic economy. But the reality for many involves a relentless hustle. The job market in desirable fields, be it tech, entertainment, or even artisanal pickle-making, can be fiercely competitive. That dream job might come with a dream commute (the kind that haunts your nightmares, see Chapter Two) or work hours that make you wonder if the sun even still exists outside your office window. The "gig economy" is a significant feature, offering flexibility but often lacking the stability and benefits of traditional employment, meaning your California dream might involve juggling multiple income streams just to keep the lights on.

Then there's the lifestyle. The California Dream often conjures images of laid-back beach vibes, endless leisure, and a general sense of "no worries." And while you can certainly find pockets of that, the reality for many, particularly in the major metropolitan areas, is a high-octane, high-stress existence. The pressure to succeed, to innovate, to keep up, can be intense. That laid-back surfer you picture might actually be a CEO who just squeezed in a dawn patrol session before a grueling day of investor meetings. The "chill" Californian might just be very good at masking their traffic-induced anxiety or their concern about the ever-present threat of earthquakes and wildfires we discussed in Chapter Five.

The dream often involves being surrounded by stunning natural beauty, and California delivers on that promise in spades. From towering redwoods to dramatic coastlines and majestic mountains, the scenery is often breathtaking. The reality, however, is that accessing this beauty can sometimes feel like a competitive sport.

138

Popular national parks can be incredibly crowded, requiring reservations months in advance. Your favorite hiking trail might resemble a conga line on a sunny Saturday. And the very environment that provides this beauty is also under significant stress from drought, wildfires, and the sheer impact of millions of people wanting a piece of it, a theme Chapter Twenty-One will explore in terms of personal safety in the outdoors.

And what about the people? The dream might be one of effortlessly blending into a community of effortlessly cool, open-minded individuals. As we explored in Chapter Fourteen, finding your tribe is crucial, but the "California Freeze" can be a real phenomenon. People are often friendly on a superficial level, but forming deep, lasting connections can take time and concerted effort. The sheer scale of the cities and the transient nature of some populations can make it harder to put down roots than you might imagine. The laid-back vibe can sometimes mask a certain reserve or a busy schedule that leaves little room for new acquaintances.

Even the "perfect weather" myth deserves a slight reality check. Yes, compared to many parts of the country, California's climate is a gift. But Southern California has its "May Gray" and "June Gloom," when the marine layer can sock in the coast for weeks. Northern California, especially San Francisco, has its famous fog, Karl, who can turn a summer day into a surprisingly chilly affair. Inland areas can experience scorching summer heat, and the entire state deals with periods of drought that impact everything from your garden to your water bill. It's not all 72 degrees and sunny, though there's certainly a generous helping of that.

The powerful "anything is possible" ethos of California is a huge part of its allure. It's a place that has always attracted dreamers, innovators, and those looking to reinvent themselves. And for many, that dream of transformation comes true. But the reality is that reinvention is hard work. Success, however you define it, rarely falls into your lap. It requires resilience, adaptability, often a bit of luck, and the ability to pick yourself up after inevitable setbacks. Not everyone strikes gold, whether that's literal gold in the 1850s or venture capital gold today. There's also a subtle pressure in some circles to project an image of constant success and happiness, which can be challenging when you're navigating the inevitable bumps in the road.

So, how do you move to California without your dream deflating like a cheap pool toy on day two? Managing expectations is your most powerful tool. This isn't about being pessimistic; it's about being realistic, which allows you to appreciate the genuine wonders of the state without being blindsided by its less-than-perfect aspects.

Before you even think about packing a single box, **do your homework, and then do some more.** Go beyond the glossy brochures and the curated Instagram feeds. Read local news from the specific areas you're considering. Peruse online forums where actual residents discuss the pros and cons of their neighborhoods. Look at cost-of-living calculators, but also delve into specific prices for things that matter to you – from childcare to your favorite brand of coffee. Understand the commute times from potential neighborhoods to potential job centers, not just in miles, but in actual, soul-crushing, rush-hour minutes.

If you can, **visit before you commit, and not just as a tourist.** Spend a week or two, if possible, living more like a local in the area you're targeting. Go grocery shopping. Try commuting during peak hours. Check out the parks, the libraries, the general vibe on a Tuesday afternoon, not just a festive Saturday night. This "test drive" can be invaluable in aligning your expectations with on-the-ground reality.

Crucially, take some time to **define what your personal California Dream actually looks like.** Is it the Hollywood version of fame and fortune? Is it about a specific career opportunity? Is it about access to nature, a particular lifestyle, or being closer to a certain community? The more specific you are about *your* priorities, the better you can assess whether a particular part of California can realistically deliver on them. Not all dreams are compatible with all locations, even within this vast state. The dream of a quiet, affordable life surrounded by nature is very different from the dream of being at the epicenter of the tech industry, and they usually don't occupy the same zip code.

One of the most important mindset shifts is to **embrace imperfection.** California is not a utopia. It has problems, just like any other place, sometimes on a grander, more dramatic scale. There will be frustrating bureaucratic encounters (as Chapters Four and Thirteen attest), days when the traffic makes you question all your life choices, and moments when the cost of a simple sandwich makes you want to weep. Learning to accept, and even find humor in, these imperfections is key to long-term contentment. California's flaws are part of its character, like the endearing eccentricities of a beloved, if occasionally infuriating, friend.

Financial realism cannot be overstated. The "Sunshine Tax" is real and relentless. Before you move, have a brutally honest look at your finances. Create a detailed budget based on California-specific costs. Have a robust emergency fund, because unexpected expenses here can be particularly un-fun. Don't assume that a higher California salary will automatically translate to a higher standard of living; it might just mean you're treading water in a more expensive pool. The dream of "making it" often starts with the reality of "making rent."

Be prepared to be **flexible and adaptable.** Your initial plan might need tweaking, or perhaps a complete overhaul, once you arrive. The job you thought was perfect might not be. The neighborhood you researched meticulously might not feel right. The dream you arrived with might evolve as you experience the reality of living here. Being open to change, willing to pivot (to borrow a term from the tech bros), and resilient in the face of challenges will serve you far better than rigid adherence to a pre-conceived notion.

So, what is the "real" California Dream, then? Perhaps it's not a single, shiny, pre-packaged ideal, but something more personal and nuanced. For many, it's found in the state's incredible diversity – of people, cultures, landscapes, and ideas. It's in the spirit of innovation and the willingness to question the status quo.

It's in the access to breathtaking natural beauty, even if you have to share it with a few million of your closest friends. It's in the perfect taco from a tiny, unassuming truck, the unexpected kindness of a stranger in a vast city, or the profound sense of peace watching the sun dip into the Pacific.

The California Dream might also be about the *pursuit* itself, the act of striving, of reaching for something more, even if the path is bumpier and the destination looks a little different than you initially imagined. It's about the personal growth that comes from navigating a complex and demanding environment. It's about discovering strengths you didn't know you had and building a life that is authentically yours, even if it doesn't perfectly match the glossy images.

Managing your expectations isn't about giving up on the dream; it's about equipping yourself with the clarity and resilience to build your own version of it, grounded in the often messy, sometimes frustrating, but ultimately rewarding reality of this extraordinary state. California has a way of testing you, challenging you, and, if you let it, changing you for the better. Approach it with open eyes, a realistic budget, a good sense of humor, and a willingness to adapt, and you might just find that your California reality, while different from the initial dream, is pretty golden after all.

CHAPTER TWENTY: Registering Your Car: Prepare for Paperwork Apocalypse

Alright, intrepid adventurer, you've scaled the precarious peaks of California housing, navigated the treacherous currents of its freeways, and perhaps even deciphered the ancient hieroglyphs of a utility bill. You might be feeling a surge of accomplishment, a sense that you're truly starting to conquer this Golden State. That's adorable. Now, allow us to introduce you to a rite of passage so profoundly Californian, so exquisitely bureaucratic, it makes the DMV visit for your driver's license (Chapter Four, remember that quaint little escapade?) look like a leisurely stroll on the beach. Welcome, dear friend, to the glorious, soul-testing, paper-strewn battlefield of registering your out-of-state vehicle in California. Prepare for the Paperwork Apocalypse.

This isn't just about getting a new license plate; it's a quest, a trial by triplicate form, a financial flagellation that will leave you questioning your life choices and the very nature of stamped, official documents. Why the drama? Because California, in its infinite wisdom and its unyielding commitment to ensuring every vehicle gracing its pristine (and occasionally potholed) roadways is properly accounted for, taxed, and smog-compliant, has crafted a process of delightful intricacy. Forget any breezy experiences you might have had registering a car in other, less administratively ambitious states. This is the big leagues of vehicular bureaucracy.

First, let's discuss the ticking clock, the gentle nudge from the state that says, "Welcome! Now give us your car's paperwork and a significant portion of your worldly wealth, and do it *yesterday*." Generally, you have **20 days** after establishing residency or becoming employed in California to register your vehicle with the Department of Motor Vehicles. What constitutes "establishing residency"? The DMV has its ways of knowing, often tied to when you get your California driver's license, rent an apartment, or start that dream job. Don't dawdle. The penalties for late registration can add an extra layer of financial ouch to an already tender situation. Procrastination is not your friend in this particular quest.

Now, before you even dream of approaching the hallowed halls of the DMV, you must embark on a sacred scavenger hunt for documents. This is where the "apocalypse" part really starts to feel accurate. You'll need an arsenal of paperwork, each piece more critical than the last. Consider this your basic loadout:

1. **Your Out-of-State Title:** This is the crown jewel, the proof that you actually own the magnificent chariot you're attempting to register. If there's a lienholder (i.e., you're still paying off a loan), you'll need the name and address of the bank or finance company. The DMV might need to request the title from them, which can add a delightful layer of suspense and delay. If your title is currently held by the lienholder in another state, you'll need to navigate that particular maze.

2. **Your Out-of-State Registration:** The current, valid registration card from your previous state is also required. This helps establish the vehicle's history and your ownership.

3. **Proof of Insurance:** You'll need to show that your vehicle is insured according to California's minimum liability requirements. Your insurance card or policy declaration page should suffice, but make sure it reflects California coverage.

4. **A California Smog Certificate:** Ah, the sweet smell of emissions compliance! As we touched upon in Chapter Thirteen regarding ongoing smog checks, California requires that most gasoline-powered vehicles being brought into the state for the first time pass a California smog inspection. It doesn't matter if your car just passed a smog test in your former state with flying colors. California has its own standards, its own tests, and its own special way of making you feel like your car is single-handedly trying to

melt the polar ice caps. You'll need to take your vehicle to a licensed California smog check station. If it fails, you'll need to get it repaired and retested before you can proceed with registration. (Electric vehicles, some hybrids, and very old vehicles might be exempt – always check the current BAR and DMV rules).

5. **The Application for Title or Registration (Form REG 343):** This is the main DMV form you'll be wrestling with. Fill it out neatly, accurately, and perhaps with a silent prayer to the patron saint of legible handwriting. It asks for all sorts of exciting details about you and your vehicle.

6. **Verification of Vehicle (Form REG 31):** This is a fun one. A DMV employee, a certified vehicle verifier (often found at private registration services or some dealerships, for a fee), or a peace officer (like the CHP) must physically inspect your vehicle to confirm that its Vehicle Identification Number (VIN) matches your paperwork and that its emissions equipment is all present and accounted for (especially important for vehicles from out of state). This isn't a mechanical inspection, just a verification that your car is, in fact, your car and has the legally required bits. Many people opt to have this done at the DMV during their registration appointment.

Depending on your specific situation, other forms might leap joyfully onto your pile. For example, a **Statement of Facts (Form REG 256)** might be needed to claim certain exemptions or clarify details. If you're dealing with a leased vehicle, you'll likely need a power of attorney from the leasing company and their specific instructions.

Once you've assembled your papyrus hoard, it's time to confront the financial dragon. Registering your car in California is not an inexpensive proposition. Be prepared for a cascade of fees, each more inventive than the last. These can include:

- **Registration Fee:** This is the basic fee to register your vehicle.

- **Vehicle License Fee (VLF):** This is the big one for many. The VLF is an ad valorem tax, meaning it's based on the current market value of your vehicle. The newer and fancier your ride, the more you'll contribute to this particular coffer. It's often the largest component of your registration costs.

- **California Highway Patrol (CHP) Fee:** A fee to help fund those friendly folks who patrol the freeways.

- **County/District Fees:** Various local fees can be tacked on, depending on where you live, often for transportation projects or air quality initiatives.

- **Smog Abatement Fee:** For newer vehicles exempt from the biennial smog check, you'll still pay this fee annually.

- **Use Tax:** This is a potential landmine for those who recently purchased their vehicle out-of-state and then brought it to California. If you paid less sales tax in the state where you bought the car than you would have paid in California, or if you bought it from a private party with no tax paid, California may assess a "use tax" based on its value to make up the difference. This can be a very significant, and often unexpected, expense. There are some exemptions, for instance, if you owned and operated the vehicle for a significant period in another state before becoming a California resident, but the rules are specific. Prepare for this possibility if your car is a recent acquisition.

Add all these up, and the grand total can easily run into many hundreds, or even thousands, of dollars, especially for newer vehicles or those subject to use tax. The DMV website usually has a fee calculator that can give you an estimate, but it's often just that – an estimate. The final, official figure will be revealed at the

DMV counter, often with a dramatic flourish (or at least, that's how it feels when you're handing over your credit card).

With your documents clutched tightly and your wallet braced for impact, it's time for the pilgrimage to the DMV. As we discussed in Chapter Four, appointments are your golden ticket to a potentially less soul-crushing experience. Book one online, well in advance if possible, specifically for vehicle registration. If you're a brave walk-in warrior, arrive early, pack snacks, and mentally prepare for a wait that could rival the gestation period of a small mammal.

When your number is finally called, approach the counter with a calm demeanor and your meticulously organized paperwork. The DMV technician will scrutinize your documents with the intensity of a diamond cutter. They'll verify your VIN (if it wasn't done beforehand), calculate your fees, and, if all is in order, accept your payment. This is the moment of truth. If there are any discrepancies, missing forms, or unpaid parking tickets from a forgotten youthful indiscretion that have somehow attached themselves to your record, you might be sent back to the drawing board, or to another, even longer, line.

Assuming you survive this gauntlet, you'll typically receive a temporary operating permit to display in your vehicle. Your new California license plates and registration stickers will usually be mailed to you within a few weeks. That temporary permit is your proof that you've appeased the DMV gods, at least for now. Guard it well. When those shiny new plates finally arrive, affixing them to your car will feel like a victory lap, a hard-won badge of honor signifying your official vehicular assimilation into the Golden State.

A few special considerations:

- **Leased Vehicles:** Registering a leased car usually requires coordination with your leasing company. They hold the title, and you'll likely need a power of attorney from them and specific forms they provide. Start this process early, as it can add time.

- **Vehicles with Out-of-State Lienholders:** If you have a loan on your car, the California DMV will need to record the lienholder information. Your out-of-state title should have this, or you may need to provide additional documentation from your lender.

- **Military Personnel:** If you're an active-duty member of the U.S. Armed Forces stationed in California, you may have options regarding vehicle registration. You might be able to maintain your home state registration, or you might qualify for certain exemptions or deferrals of California registration fees, like the VLF, if you choose to register here. Specific forms and documentation (like your military ID and official orders) will be required. The rules are detailed, so check with the DMV or your base legal assistance office.

- **Non-Resident Vehicles:** If you are a true non-resident – for example, a student attending a California university but maintaining residency in another state, or on a temporary work assignment with no intent to establish residency – you might not be required to register your vehicle in California, provided it remains currently registered in your home state and you meet specific criteria. However, the moment you accept gainful employment or take other steps to establish residency, that 20-day clock generally starts ticking.

The process of registering your out-of-state vehicle in California is undeniably a bureaucratic marathon. It's designed to be thorough, and it often feels like it's designed to test the very limits of your patience and your checkbook. But it's a necessary hurdle. Having your vehicle legally registered in California, with California plates and current tags, is essential for avoiding hefty fines, potential impoundment, and the general inconvenience of being on the wrong side of the law.

Once it's done, once those plates are on and the paperwork is filed away (in a very safe place, because you never know when you might need to prove you survived this), there's a profound sense of relief. You've conquered another layer of California bureaucracy. You've paid your dues (literally). Your car is now an official, tax-paying, smog-compliant Californian, just like you're aspiring to be. Now, if you could just find a decent parking spot… but that's a challenge for another day. For now, revel in your victory over the paperwork apocalypse. You've earned it. And remember, always check the official DMV website for the most current forms, fees, and procedures. They change, because California.

CHAPTER TWENTY-ONE: The Great Outdoors: Avoiding Rattlesnakes and Poison Oak

So, you've started to explore California's magnificent outdoors, as discussed back in Chapter Eight. You've got your hiking boots, your reusable water bottle adorned with stickers from places you haven't actually visited yet, and a burgeoning appreciation for landscapes that don't involve concrete. Wonderful! Now, let's talk about some of the... *spicier* elements of Mother Nature's welcoming committee here in the Golden State. Beyond the awe-inspiring vistas and the soul-soothing tranquility, there are a few residents and botanical features that prefer you keep a respectful, and occasionally panicked, distance. We're not trying to scare you back into your overpriced apartment, but a little knowledge can go a long way in ensuring your outdoor adventures remain memorable for the right reasons, rather than for an unscheduled trip to the emergency room or a week of itching that makes you question your life choices.

First on our hit parade of things to politely avoid is the **rattlesnake**. Yes, these venomous pit vipers are card-carrying Californians, found in a variety of habitats from coastal scrub and grasslands to deserts and forests, generally from sea level up to around 11,000 feet. There are several species here, including the Northern Pacific, Southern Pacific, Western Diamondback, Sidewinder, Mojave, and a few others. Identifying them usually isn't too tricky: they have that characteristic triangular head, often a somewhat stocky body with blotchy patterns, and, of course, the eponymous rattle at the end of their tail (though baby rattlesnakes might only have a "button" and not much of a rattle, and sometimes adult snakes lose their rattles or don't rattle before striking).

Rattlesnakes are not inherently aggressive; they'd much rather avoid you than engage. They bite out of self-defense when they feel threatened or surprised. The key is to give them a wide berth. Most bites occur when people accidentally step on or near them, or try to handle or harass them (pro tip: don't do that). They are most active in warmer weather – spring, summer, and early fall – and often bask in sunny spots in the morning or seek shade during the hottest part of the day. They can also be active at night during hot periods.

So, how do you avoid an unpleasant tête-à-tête? First, be aware of your surroundings, especially when hiking or in areas where they might be present. Stick to cleared trails as much as possible. Avoid walking through tall grass or dense brush where you can't see your feet. Never put your hands or feet where you can't see, like into rock crevices, under logs, or into thick bushes. If you're scrambling over rocks or logs, look first. Wear sturdy, over-the-ankle hiking boots and loose-fitting long pants, which can offer some protection. Make noise while you walk; the vibrations can alert snakes to your presence, giving them a chance to move away. If you hear a rattle, freeze! Locate the snake, then slowly back away and give it plenty of room to retreat or go around it at a very safe distance. Do not try to poke it, throw things at it, or take a super-close selfie. This is not the time for Instagram heroics.

What if, despite your best efforts, the unthinkable happens and you or someone with you is bitten? **Seek immediate medical attention.** Call 911 or get to the nearest emergency room as quickly and safely as possible. Keep the bitten limb below the level of the heart if possible and try to remain calm (easier said than done, we know). Remove any tight clothing or jewelry near the bite site, as swelling will occur. Do **NOT** apply a tourniquet. Do **NOT** cut the wound and try to suck out the venom (this is movie stuff, and it's harmful). Do **NOT** apply ice or heat. Do **NOT** give the victim alcohol or caffeine. The only effective treatment for a venomous snakebite is antivenom, administered by medical professionals. Remember the snake's appearance if you can, but don't try to catch or kill it; that just risks another bite. Most rattlesnake bites are survivable with prompt medical care.

Now, let's move from slithering surprises to botanical bothers, specifically the undisputed champion of Californian itchiness: **poison oak**. *Toxicodendron diversilobum* is a master of disguise and a prolific resident of woodlands, grasslands, chaparral, and even some coastal areas. It can grow as a ground vine, a shrub, or a climbing vine that shimmies up trees with impressive determination. Its motto is "leaves of three, let it be," which is a good starting point, but its appearance can vary maddeningly. The leaves are typically lobed or toothed, somewhat resembling oak leaves (hence the name), and can be glossy or dull, green in spring and summer, and then turn spectacular shades of red, orange, or yellow in the fall before dropping off. Even the bare stems in winter can still carry the urushiol oil that causes the infamous rash.

Urushiol is the oily culprit responsible for the intensely itchy, blistering rash that can make you want to claw your skin off with a rusty garden rake. You can get it by directly brushing against any part of the plant, by touching clothing or tools that have urushiol on them, or even from petting an animal that has recently romped through a patch. Smoke from burning poison oak is also incredibly hazardous if inhaled and can cause severe respiratory issues and systemic reactions. So, if you're clearing brush, know what you're dealing with before you toss it on a bonfire.

How to avoid this botanical menace? Learn to identify it in all its seasonal finery. Seriously, study pictures, ask experienced hikers to point it out. Stay on trails. Wear long pants, long sleeves, and closed shoes if you're hiking in areas where it's prevalent. Consider using a barrier cream like IvyX or Tecnu on exposed skin before heading out, though these aren't foolproof. If you think you've made contact, wash the affected skin as soon as possible (within 10-20 minutes is best, but even later can help) with cool water and soap (dish soap is good for cutting through oil) or a specialized poison oak cleanser like Tecnu or Zanfel. Clean under your fingernails. Carefully remove and wash any clothing, shoes, or gear that might have touched the plant, as urushiol can remain active for a long time.

If you do get the rash, welcome to the club. It typically appears within 12 to 72 hours after exposure and can last for one to three weeks, or even longer in severe cases. Try not to scratch (again, easier said than done), as this can lead to infection. Cool compresses, calamine lotion, oatmeal baths, and over-the-counter hydrocortisone creams can help soothe the itching. For severe reactions, widespread rashes, or involvement of the face, eyes, or genitals, see a doctor. They may prescribe stronger topical steroids or oral corticosteroids. The good news? You're not contagious to others once you've washed the urushiol off your skin, though you can re-contaminate yourself from oil still on clothing or tools.

Beyond our headliners, California's great outdoors hosts a few other characters worth knowing. **Ticks** are tiny arachnids that love to hang out in grassy, brushy, or wooded areas, waiting for a warm-blooded host (like you or your dog) to wander by. They can transmit diseases, most notably Lyme disease, but also others like Rocky Mountain spotted fever and anaplasmosis. Lyme disease is present in California, particularly in the coastal counties and the Sierra Nevada foothills. Not all ticks carry diseases, but it's wise to take precautions. Use an EPA-registered insect repellent effective against ticks (containing DEET, picaridin, or oil of lemon eucalyptus). Wear light-colored clothing so ticks are easier to spot. Tuck your pant legs into your socks if you're in a tick-heavy area (you might look like a dork, but it's better than Lyme). Stay in the center of trails. After your outing, do a thorough tick check on yourself, your kids, and your pets. Pay attention to your scalp, ears, armpits, groin, and behind your knees. If you find an embedded tick, remove it carefully with fine-tipped tweezers, grasping as close to the skin as possible and pulling straight out without twisting or jerking. Clean the bite area and your hands. If you develop a rash (especially a bull's-eye rash, a hallmark of Lyme) or flu-like symptoms after a tick bite, see your doctor promptly.

Spiders like the **black widow** (identifiable by the red hourglass on the underside of its abdomen) and, less commonly encountered but still present, the **brown recluse** (with its violin-shaped marking on its back) can be found in California, often in undisturbed places like woodpiles, sheds, garages, and sometimes outdoor furniture or clutter. Their bites can be serious. Be cautious when reaching into dark, cluttered spaces. If bitten, seek medical attention. Scorpions are also present, especially in desert and arid regions. Most California scorpion stings are painful but not life-threatening, akin to a bee sting, but the bark scorpion (found in some far southeastern desert areas) has a more potent venom. Again, shaking out shoes and clothing before putting them on if you're in scorpion country is a good habit.

While Chapter Five covered larger-scale natural events, when you're out in the wilderness, especially in more remote areas, awareness of larger wildlife is prudent. **Mountain lions** (also called cougars or pumas) are elusive and generally avoid humans, but encounters can occur, especially in areas where development encroaches on their habitat. If you see one, do not approach it. Make yourself appear as large as possible, make noise, and slowly back away. Do not run, as this can trigger their prey drive. Keep children close. **Black bears** are also found in many mountainous and forested areas. Proper food storage is crucial when camping (use bear lockers or bear canisters). Make noise while hiking to avoid surprising a bear. If you encounter one, again, make yourself look big, make noise, and back away slowly. Never feed bears or other wildlife.

Let's not forget our coastal critters. If you're enjoying California's beautiful beaches, particularly in Southern California, learn the "stingray shuffle." Wading into the water, shuffle your feet along the sandy bottom. This alerts any stingrays resting there to your presence, giving them a chance to swim away. Stepping directly on one can result in a painful sting from the barb on its tail. If you are stung, soaking the affected area in hot water (as hot as you can tolerate without burning) can help denature the venom and reduce pain, but a medical evaluation is still a good idea, especially if the barb breaks off in the wound. **Jellyfish** can also make an appearance, especially during certain times of the year. Their stings can be painful. Heed any posted warnings. Vinegar is often recommended for some types of jellyfish stings to neutralize the stinging cells, but avoid rubbing the area.

154

Some other plants to be aware of include **stinging nettle**, which has fine hairs that inject irritating chemicals when touched, causing a burning, stinging sensation and a temporary rash. It's often found in moist, shady areas. The discomfort usually subsides within a few hours. And, especially in areas recovering from wildfires, you might encounter **poodle-dog bush**, a plant whose sticky hairs can cause a severe skin irritation similar to or even worse than poison oak for some people. It's another one to learn to identify and avoid.

Finally, while it might seem obvious, the California sun and varied terrain demand respect. **Sunburn and heat exhaustion/heatstroke** are real risks, especially in the deserts or during summer hikes at lower elevations. Wear sunscreen, a wide-brimmed hat, and sunglasses. Carry and drink plenty of water – more than you think you'll need. Dehydration can sneak up on you quickly. Tell someone where you're going and when you expect to be back, especially if you're hiking alone. Carry a basic first-aid kit, a map (don't rely solely on your phone's GPS, as service can be spotty), and appropriate layers of clothing, as weather can change rapidly, especially in the mountains or on the coast.

This might all sound like a gauntlet of natural perils designed to keep you cowering indoors. But that's not the intent. Millions of Californians enjoy the state's incredible natural beauty every year without incident. The key is awareness, preparedness, and a healthy dose of respect for the wilder side of the Golden State. By learning to recognize and avoid these potential hazards, you can explore with confidence, knowing you're equipped to handle (or better yet, sidestep) the less-than-cuddly aspects of California's great outdoors. Now, go forth and explore (cautiously, and with plenty of anti-itch cream in your backpack, just in case).

CHAPTER TWENTY-TWO: Joining the Cult: Fitness Trends and Wellness Obsessions

Alright, future Californian, you've unpacked your boxes (mostly), figured out which freeway goes in vaguely the right direction (sometimes), and you're starting to suspect that "avocado" is less a fruit and more a primary food group here. Excellent. Now, it's time to address a rather prominent feature of the Golden State's cultural landscape, one that can be as alluring as it is occasionally intimidating: the relentless pursuit of fitness and wellness. Welcome, initiate, to the many and varied "cults" of California health. We use the term "cult" loosely, of course, with a hefty dose of affection and a knowing wink. But let's be honest, when your neighbor starts referring to their spin instructor as their "guru" and their pre-dawn workout as a "sacred ritual," you might start to wonder if you've accidentally stumbled into a very well-hydrated, Lululemon-clad sect.

In California, fitness isn't just something you *do*; it's often something you *are*. It's woven into the social fabric, the professional networking scene, and even the way people dress for a trip to the grocery store. The sheer variety of ways to sweat, stretch, and "optimize your vessel" can be downright dizzying. It's a state where finding your "fitness tribe" can be as crucial as finding a decent taco truck (though arguably, the latter is a more straightforward quest). So, grab your reusable water bottle (preferably one that makes a statement), and let's explore the beautifully sculpted, occasionally perplexing, world of California's fitness and wellness obsessions.

The most obvious entry point into this world is the ubiquitous **gym culture**. California boasts an almost comical density of fitness facilities. You've got your big-box chains like 24 Hour Fitness or LA Fitness, veritable cathedrals of cardio equipment and weight machines, often bustling at all hours. Then there are the more upscale athletic clubs, sometimes resembling five-star resorts with valet parking, spas, and cafes serving kale smoothies that cost more than your monthly streaming subscriptions. But beyond these generalists, California is the spiritual homeland of the **boutique fitness studio**, where specialization is key and a sense of community (or, yes, "cult") is carefully cultivated.

Prepare yourself for the phenomenon of the **spin class**. Places like SoulCycle and its many disciples have transformed stationary cycling into a quasi-spiritual experience, complete with dimly lit rooms, pumping music, inspirational mantras shouted by charismatic instructors, and a price point per class that might make you briefly consider taking up jogging (which, by the way, is also a very serious cult here). It's less a workout and more a sweaty, cathartic dance party on a bike, often with a dedicated following who book their preferred bikes and instructors with the fervor of concert-goers vying for front-row tickets.

Then there's **yoga**, which in California has mutated and multiplied into more forms than there are varieties of artisanal kombucha. You've got your traditional Hatha and Vinyasa, of course, but why stop there? There's Bikram or "hot yoga," practiced in rooms heated to sweat-lodge temperatures, promising detoxification and a flexibility you didn't know your hamstrings possessed. There's aerial yoga, where you perform poses while suspended in silk hammocks, looking like a very graceful (or occasionally very tangled) Cirque du Soleil performer. There's paddleboard yoga (SUP yoga), because balancing on solid ground was clearly too easy. And yes, goat yoga is a real thing – tiny, adorable goats frolicking around (and sometimes on) you as you attempt a downward-facing dog. The quest for inner peace, it seems, is often accompanied by a desire for a novel Instagram post.

Pilates studios, with their gleaming, slightly medieval-looking Reformer machines, are another fixture. These promise long, lean muscles and a core strength that could withstand a minor earthquake. Mat classes are also popular, often held in serene, light-filled spaces. And let's not forget **Barre**, the ballet-inspired workout that involves tiny, pulsing movements at a ballet barre, leaving your muscles trembling and your respect for professional dancers exponentially increased. These classes often attract a fiercely loyal clientele who swear by their transformative, thigh-quivering power.

For those who prefer their fitness with a side of friendly competition and a timer, **High-Intensity Interval Training (HIIT)** studios are booming. Places like Orangetheory Fitness, with its heart-rate-monitor-driven workouts, or Barry's Bootcamp, with its red-lit rooms and treadmill-and-weights formula, promise maximum calorie burn in minimum time. The atmosphere is energetic, often loud, and designed to push you to your limits. Similarly, **CrossFit** "boxes" (they're not called gyms) have carved out a significant niche, fostering incredibly tight-knit communities built around constantly varied, high-intensity functional movements. Expect to learn a whole new vocabulary (WODs, AMRAPs, kipping pull-ups) and witness feats of strength that will make you reconsider your definition of "fit."

Of course, in a state blessed with such abundant natural beauty (as discussed in Chapters Eight and Twenty-One), a huge amount of California's fitness culture spills outdoors. **Running clubs** are legion, catering to everyone from casual joggers to serious marathoners. Training for iconic races like the LA Marathon, the San Francisco Marathon, or the quirky Bay to Breakers (a costumed run across San Francisco) is a major commitment and a significant social activity for many. The sight of color-coordinated groups pounding the pavement along beach paths or park trails is a daily Californian spectacle.

Hiking, as we've established, is practically a state religion, but it often transcends mere leisure and becomes a dedicated fitness pursuit. The "athleisure" uniform – stylish leggings, high-performance tops, trail running shoes, and a hydration pack – is de rigueur. Weekend mornings see trailheads bustling with an energy that rivals a popular brunch spot. It's as much about the workout and the views as it is about the social aspect of conquering a peak with your equally breathless companions.

And then there's the **beach workout** scene, particularly vibrant in Southern California. From organized bootcamps on the sand, where instructors bark orders over the sound of crashing waves, to the legendary Muscle Beach in Venice, with its outdoor weightlifting platforms and a colorful cast of characters, the coastline itself becomes an open-air gym. You'll see people practicing acroyoga, slacklining between palm trees, or simply going for a grueling run on the soft sand.

The **cycling culture** is equally fervent. Lycra-clad road cyclists are a common sight, tackling challenging coastal routes like Highway 1 or climbing steep mountain passes. Mountain bikers explore the state's vast network of trails, from flowing singletrack to technical descents. Organized group rides and charity cycling events are popular, fostering a strong sense of camaraderie among those who love to explore on two wheels.

Beyond the purely physical, California is ground zero for the **wellness industrial complex**. This is where fitness bleeds into a broader obsession with optimizing every aspect of one's being. **Juice cleanses and detoxes** are a rite of passage for some, with dedicated juice bars on seemingly every corner, offering vibrant concoctions of pressed fruits and vegetables that promise to purify your soul (and empty your wallet). The vocabulary of dietary tribes is spoken fluently here: organic, vegan, gluten-free, keto, paleo, raw. Restaurants proudly display these labels, and dinner party conversations can sometimes devolve into passionate debates about the merits of different eating philosophies.

The quest for wellness often extends into the realm of **supplements and "biohacking,"** particularly in tech-centric areas like Silicon Valley. Here, optimizing cognitive function and physical performance through carefully curated regimens of vitamins, nootropics, and sometimes more experimental interventions is not uncommon. The language of efficiency and data analysis is applied to the human body itself. This blends seamlessly with the rise of **meditation and mindfulness**. While rooted in ancient practices, mindfulness has been thoroughly modernized and often tech-enabled, with a plethora of apps, online courses, and chic urban meditation studios offering guided sessions to help stressed-out Californians find their center, even if it's just for twenty minutes between meetings.

Alternative therapies are also deeply ingrained in the California wellness landscape. Acupuncture, cupping (those circular bruises on athletes aren't from alien encounters), reiki, naturopathy, and chiropractic care are widely accepted and utilized. Newer trends like cryotherapy (exposing the body to extremely cold temperatures for purported health benefits) and float tanks (sensory deprivation tanks filled with Epsom salt-saturated water) cater to those seeking the cutting edge of recovery and relaxation. And for a more immersive experience, **wellness retreats** – often set in stunning natural locations like Big Sur or the desert – offer curated programs of yoga, meditation, healthy eating, and various healing modalities, promising a complete physical and spiritual reset, for a price.

Naturally, looking the part is almost as important as playing the part. California has arguably driven the global trend of **high-end activewear as everyday attire.** Brands like Lululemon, Alo Yoga, Outdoor Voices, and Vuori are not just for the gym; they're for brunch, for errands, for school drop-off, for pretty much any occasion short of a black-tie gala (and even then, someone might try it). Investing in the "right" gear for your chosen fitness cult – the specific cycling shoes, the yoga mat made from sustainable unicorn tears, the trail running vest with a thousand tiny pockets – is often part of the initiation. Even your water bottle can be a status symbol, a carefully chosen accessory that signals your commitment to hydration and your aesthetic sensibilities.

This intense focus on fitness and wellness inevitably has a strong **social component**. Joining a boutique fitness class, a running club, or a CrossFit box isn't just about the workout; it's about finding your community, your "fit fam." These groups often organize social events outside of their sweat sessions, from post-workout brunches to weekend retreats. For many newcomers to California, shared fitness pursuits become a primary way to meet people and build a social network. Dating apps even have filters for fitness levels, and "let's go for a hike" is a perfectly acceptable first date suggestion.

This pervasive culture can, for some, create a certain **pressure to participate**, or at least to project an image of health and vitality. In a state where it often feels like everyone is training for a marathon, subsisting on green juice, or emerging from a hot yoga class looking enviably glowy, it's easy to feel like a slacker if your primary form of exercise is walking to the fridge. The "California body" ideal, often portrayed in media as lean, toned, and perpetually tan, can also contribute to body image pressures. It's important to find a balance that feels authentic and sustainable for you, rather than succumbing to the pressure to conform to an often-unattainable ideal.

While these trends are widespread, there are subtle **regional variations**. Southern California, with its Hollywood influence and beach-centric lifestyle, might place a stronger emphasis on aesthetics and the "see and be seen" aspect of fitness culture. Think Muscle Beach, the rollerbladers of Venice, and the sheer number of juice bars per capita in Santa Monica. Northern California, particularly the Bay Area, might lean more towards performance-oriented fitness that complements an outdoorsy lifestyle (hiking, trail running, cycling) or tech-driven wellness (biohacking, meditation apps). But these are broad generalizations, and you'll find every flavor of fitness fanatic throughout the state.

And, of course, there's the **cost factor**. As we bemoaned in Chapter Nine, California living isn't cheap, and its fitness and wellness obsessions are no exception. Those boutique fitness classes can easily run $30-$40 a pop. A month's supply of organic, cold-pressed juice can cost more than a car payment. High-quality activewear is an investment. While there are certainly more affordable ways to stay active – running outdoors, hiking local trails, utilizing free community workout programs – the prevailing aspirational fitness culture often comes with a premium price tag.

Ultimately, navigating California's fitness and wellness landscape is about finding what genuinely makes you feel good, both physically and mentally. Whether you fully immerse yourself in a specific "cult," dabble in a few different trends, or simply enjoy observing the spectacle from the sidelines with an In-N-Out burger in hand, there's no one "right" way to do it. The beauty of California is the sheer abundance of choice. You can find your tribe of ultra-marathoners, your community of contemplative yogis, or simply a pleasant park path for your daily constitutional. Just remember to stay hydrated, listen to your body, and don't be surprised if you suddenly develop very strong opinions about the best brand of kombucha. It's all part of becoming a Californian.

CHAPTER TWENTY-THREE: Taxes, Taxes, and More Taxes (Welcome to the Club!)

Well, look at you, intrepid settler. You've braved the freeways, found a dwelling that doesn't (entirely) resemble a hobbit hole, and maybe even figured out how to correctly sort your kombucha bottles for recycling. You're practically a Californian! Now, allow us to usher you into the inner sanctum, the exclusive club where every resident holds a lifetime, non-transferable membership: the thrilling world of California taxes. If you thought the rent was high, just wait until you get acquainted with the various and sundry ways the Golden State requests (nay, demands) a slice of your hard-earned pie. Consider this chapter your initiation, a gentle (ish) immersion into a topic that can make even seasoned locals weep into their artisanal tax forms.

First, a word of profound, almost spiritual, importance, one that echoes the wisdom imparted in our introduction: **Tax laws and regulations are to California what Karl the Fog is to San Francisco – ever-present, occasionally obscuring, and subject to change with little warning.** What you read here is a snapshot, a general lay of the land. For the most current, accurate, and legally binding information, you must, repeat *must*, consult the official oracle: the California Franchise Tax Board (FTB) for state income taxes, the California Department of Tax and Fee Administration (CDTFA) for sales and use taxes, your local county assessor for property taxes, and the Employment Development Department (EDD) for payroll taxes like State Disability Insurance. Their websites are your new sacred texts. Bookmark them. Read them. Maybe even offer them a small, symbolic sacrifice of your spare change.

Now, let's dive into the big one, the tax that often elicits the most gasps from newcomers accustomed to gentler fiscal climates: the **California State Income Tax**. Unlike a handful of states that believe income tax is a charmingly antiquated notion, California embraces it with gusto. It's a progressive tax system, which, in layman's terms, means the more you earn, the higher the percentage of your income you'll pay in state income tax. The state has a series of tax brackets, and as your taxable income climbs through these brackets, the marginal tax rate on the income within each new bracket increases. The top marginal rates in California are among the highest in the nation, a fact that local news outlets and disgruntled former residents love to trumpet.

If you become a California resident, you are generally taxed on *all* your income, regardless of where it's earned. Yes, that includes the income from that rental property you still own back in Poughkeepsie or the freelance gig you did for a client in another country. This "worldwide income" concept can be a surprise for some. Part-year residents – those who move into or out of California during the tax year – will have a more complicated calculation, generally paying California tax on income earned while a resident and on California-sourced income earned while a non-resident. Non-residents who earn income from California sources (like working temporarily in the state or receiving rental income from a California property) will also need to file.

Filing your California state income tax return (Form 540 for full-year residents, Form 540NR for part-year residents and non-residents) can sometimes feel like an exercise in advanced algebra, especially since California tax law doesn't always conform to federal tax law. While many deductions and credits mirror the federal system, there are uniquely Californian adjustments, additions, and subtractions. For example, California has its own standard deduction amounts, and certain federal deductions might not be allowed for state purposes, or vice-versa. The Franchise Tax Board issues detailed instructions and publications each year, which are surprisingly readable if you're armed with enough caffeine and a strong will to live.

There are some California-specific tax credits you might encounter, such as the renter's credit (a modest, non-refundable credit for eligible renters meeting certain income limits), or credits for adoption expenses, and sometimes for specific energy-efficient home improvements or vehicle purchases, though these can change frequently. Don't expect these to drastically reduce your tax bill, but every little bit helps. The filing deadline for California state income taxes typically aligns with the federal deadline (usually April 15th), and extensions are available, though an extension to file is not an extension to pay any tax due.

Next, let's revisit a topic briefly touched upon in Chapter Nine: **Sales and Use Tax**. You're already familiar with sales tax being added to most purchases you make in California. The statewide base rate is set by the legislature, but cities and counties can (and enthusiastically do) add their own local sales taxes, meaning the actual rate you pay will vary depending on where you're shopping. You'll quickly learn which neighboring town has a slightly lower sales tax rate when planning a big purchase, though the savings rarely justify a cross-county expedition.

The less-understood cousin of sales tax is **Use Tax**. This is a tax on items that you purchase from an out-of-state seller for use in California, upon which California sales tax was not collected. Think online purchases from retailers who don't have a presence in California and therefore don't collect California sales tax, or items you bought in another state with a lower (or no) sales tax rate just before moving to California. The idea is to level the playing field for California businesses and ensure the state gets its due. If you owe use tax, you're generally supposed to report it and pay it with your state income tax return, or directly to the CDTFA. The state has become increasingly sophisticated at tracking these things, so ignoring it is, shall we say, ill-advised. This is particularly relevant for new residents who might ship a household full of recently purchased goods into the state.

Then there's the joy of **Property Taxes**, a significant ongoing expense for California homeowners, as Chapter Nine forewarned. The foundational principle here is **Proposition 13**, a landmark 1978 initiative that significantly reshaped California's property tax system. For existing homeowners, Prop 13 limits the annual increase in the assessed value of their property to a maximum of

2% per year (plus any voter-approved local bonds or assessments), as long as the property isn't sold or doesn't undergo major new construction. However, when a property is sold, it is reassessed at its current market value at the time of sale. For you, the happy new California homeowner who just paid a king's ransom for your slice of the dream, this means your initial property tax bill will be based on that (likely very high) purchase price. While your *rate* of increase will be limited by Prop 13 going forward, you're starting from a potentially much higher base than your neighbor who bought their house in 1975 and is still paying taxes based on an assessed value that makes you want to cry. This creates some interesting neighborhood dynamics and is a frequent topic of political debate.

Be prepared for a **supplemental property tax bill** after you purchase your home. This is a one-time bill that covers the difference between the seller's old assessed value and your new assessed value for the period between when you bought the house and the next regular property tax billing cycle. It often catches new homeowners by surprise, arriving months after they've settled in and started to breathe again financially. Property tax bills are typically paid in two installments, due November 1st and February 1st, and become delinquent after December 10th and April 10th, respectively. Remember those dates. Your county assessor and tax collector will become your new pen pals.

Beyond these titans of taxation, California has a few other unique ways to lighten your wallet. If you're employed, you'll notice a deduction on your paycheck for **State Disability Insurance (SDI)**. This is a state-mandated employee-funded program that provides short-term Disability Insurance (DI) and Paid Family Leave (PFL) wage replacement benefits to eligible workers who need to take time off work due to their own non-work-related illness or injury, or to bond with a new child or care for a seriously ill family member. While it's another deduction, it's also a valuable safety net that isn't available in all states.

We've sung the praises (or lamented the cost) of the **Vehicle License Fee (VLF)** in Chapter Twenty when discussing car registration. Remember, this is an ongoing annual fee, essentially a property tax on your vehicle, based on its current market value. It's part of your annual vehicle registration renewal bill from the DMV and can be a substantial chunk of change, especially for newer or more valuable cars. And while we're on the subject of vehicles, California's **gasoline taxes** are among the highest in the nation, as noted in Chapter Nine. This isn't a direct bill you pay, but it's built into the price at the pump and significantly contributes to the high cost of driving in the state. These funds are generally earmarked for transportation infrastructure.

If you're brave enough to start your own business or dive into the vibrant world of freelancing (as discussed in Chapter Three), you'll unlock a whole new level of tax adventure. California has been particularly active in defining who qualifies as an **independent contractor versus an employee (think Assembly Bill 5, or AB5)**, which has significant tax implications. If you're genuinely self-employed, you'll be responsible for federal self-employment taxes (Social Security and Medicare) and will likely need to make **estimated quarterly tax payments** to both the IRS and the California Franchise Tax Board to cover your income tax liability throughout the year, since you won't have an employer withholding it for you. Keeping meticulous records of income and expenses becomes not just good practice, but essential for survival. Some cities and counties also levy **local business taxes** or require business licenses, adding another layer to your fiscal fun.

For those indulging in some of California's more recently legalized recreational pursuits, be aware of **cannabis taxes**. The state levies taxes at various stages, from cultivation to retail sale. Consumers will see a hefty excise tax (and often local cannabis business taxes) built into the retail price, making legal cannabis significantly more expensive than it might be in the illicit market. These tax revenues are earmarked for various state programs, including youth education, environmental cleanup, and public safety.

The cumulative effect of all these taxes can sometimes lead to what might be affectionately termed the "Welcome to California" tax bill, especially for those moving from states with no income tax or significantly lower overall tax burdens. Your first California state income tax return can be a sobering experience if you haven't planned for it. Ensuring you have adequate withholding from your paycheck if you're an employee, or making sufficient estimated tax payments if you're self-employed, is crucial to avoid a nasty surprise (and potential underpayment penalties) come tax time.

Navigating this complex tax landscape can be daunting. The Franchise Tax Board (FTB) website (www.ftb.ca.gov) is an invaluable resource, offering forms, publications, online calculators, and answers to frequently asked questions. They also have taxpayer assistance services. For sales and use tax questions, the California Department of Tax and Fee Administration (CDTFA) website (www.cdtfa.ca.gov) is your go-to. Your local county assessor's office will have all the details on property taxes.

There comes a point, however, when DIY tax preparation might feel like trying to perform surgery on yourself with a butter knife. If your tax situation is complex – perhaps you moved mid-year, have income from multiple states, deal with stock options (a common feature in California's tech industry), own rental properties, or are self-employed with a thriving (or struggling) business – it is often well worth the expense to seek out a **qualified tax professional**. Look for an Enrolled Agent (EA), a Certified Public Accountant (CPA), or a tax attorney who is experienced specifically with California tax law, as its nuances can trip up even those familiar with federal taxes. For individuals and families with modest incomes, free tax preparation assistance is often available through programs like Volunteer Income Tax Assistance (VITA) and Tax Counseling for the Elderly (TCE).

California's tax system is intricate, reflecting the complexity and scale of the state's economy and its commitment to funding a wide array of public services, from schools and infrastructure to environmental protection and social programs. While no one particularly enjoys paying taxes, understanding the system, knowing your obligations, and planning accordingly can make the process significantly less painful. So, gather your W-2s, your 1099s, your receipts for deductible expenses (if you itemize), and perhaps a very large bottle of your preferred analgesic. Welcome to the club. Membership is mandatory, but at least the sunshine is (mostly) free.

CHAPTER TWENTY-FOUR: Learning to Love (or Tolerate) the Traffic Report

Alright, future Californian, let's have a heart-to-heart. We've navigated the labyrinthine freeways in Chapter Two, discussing the art of the merge and the existential dread of rush hour. We've even touched upon the glorious, soul-crushing SigAlert. But driving *in* California traffic is only half the battle. The other half, the one that often dictates your mood before you even grab your car keys, is understanding, interpreting, and developing a deeply personal relationship with the **California traffic report**. This isn't just a news segment; it's a daily ritual, a constant companion, a Greek chorus commentating on the collective vehicular drama of the Golden State. Learning to decipher its pronouncements, its coded language, and its often-understated delivery of truly harrowing news is a crucial step in your assimilation. Think of it as learning a new, slightly depressing, but utterly essential dialect.

The traffic report in California is an institution, as deeply ingrained in the local culture as avocado toast or complaining about the price of gas. It's the soundtrack to countless breakfasts, the decider of departure times, and the source of a million muttered curses. For many, it's the first voice they hear in the morning and the last thing they check before heading home. It's a shared experience that binds millions of Californians together in a collective groan of "Oh, not the 405 again." There's a certain camaraderie in knowing that countless others are also staring at their radios or phones, contemplating the vehicular battlefield that lies ahead.

So, where does one partake in this daily dose of commuter clairvoyance? The classic delivery system is, of course, the **radio**. Many AM stations, particularly in major metropolitan areas, are veritable firehoses of news, weather, and, most importantly, traffic. Stations like KFI AM 640 or KNX 1070 Newsradio in Southern California, and KCBS AM 740 in Northern California, provide traffic updates with astonishing frequency, often "on the eights," "on the fives," or even more frequently during peak commute times. You'll learn the rhythm: the jingle, the reporter's familiar voice, and then the litany of delays, accidents, and SigAlerts. Some stations even dedicate entire blocks of time to traffic coverage. It's a constant, soothing (or terrifying) hum in the background of many a Californian's life.

Television news also plays its part, especially during morning and evening broadcasts. Here, you get the added bonus of flashy graphics, color-coded maps showing angry red lines snaking across familiar freeways, and earnest reporters standing in front of live shots of... well, stuck traffic. The visuals can be compelling, either confirming your worst fears or offering a glimmer of hope that your particular route looks surprisingly green (a rare and beautiful sight, to be cherished).

But let's be honest, the modern Californian's traffic oracle often lives in their pocket. **Traffic apps** have revolutionized the game. Waze, with its crowd-sourced alerts on everything from accidents to potholes to police presence, offers a real-time, dynamic view of the chaos. Google Maps and Apple Maps provide constantly updated ETAs that factor in current conditions, often suggesting alternate routes that may or may not save you any actual time but will at least make you feel like you're being proactive. Dedicated apps like Sigalert.com (yes, the legend has its own app) provide focused information on major incidents. These tools have shifted the power dynamic slightly, allowing drivers to make more informed (or at least, more data-driven) decisions, rather than relying solely on the periodic updates from broadcast media.

For the truly dedicated (or professionally obligated), the **California Department of Transportation (Caltrans)** offers its own suite of information. The Caltrans QuickMap website and app provide real-time traffic information, including speeds, incidents, lane closures, and even views from traffic cameras. It's the official source, the raw data from which many other reports are derived, and can be invaluable for a deep dive into the state of the roadways.

Now, let's get to the fun part: deciphering the unique lingo of the California traffic report. It's a language honed by years of describing fender-benders and soul-crushing standstills. Knowing these terms is key to understanding just how much trouble you're in. As we've touched upon before, **freeway names and numbers** are fundamental. In Southern California, you'll hear "the 101," "the 405," "the 5," while Northern Californians will typically just say "101," "880," "580." Knowing the local freeway names – the Hollywood Freeway (US-101 in LA), the San Diego Freeway (I-405), the Bayshore Freeway (US-101 on the Peninsula), the Nimitz (I-880) – is also crucial for following along. A reporter might say, "We've got a SigAlert on the northbound Hollywood at Vine," and you're expected to know exactly where that impending doom is located.

A **SigAlert**, as we know from Chapter Two, is an unplanned event closing at least one lane for 30 minutes or more. When you hear this magic word in a traffic report, pay attention. It's the traffic reporter's equivalent of raising a giant red flag. It means something significant is afoot, and your commute is likely about to get significantly more "interesting." The report will usually specify the location, the cause (accident, overturned vehicle, emergency roadwork), and which lanes are affected.

When the freeways become impassable parking lots, traffic reports will inevitably turn to **surface streets**. These are the regular city roads, the arterials and boulevards that become the reluctant escape valves for freeway refugees. You'll hear things like, "Sepulveda is jammed as an alternate for the 405," or "Avoid El Camino Real; it's seeing heavy spillover from 101." Knowing the major surface street alternatives in your area can be a lifesaver, though often these routes become just as congested as the freeways they're meant to relieve.

Then there are the common phrases, the everyday poetry of the traffic report:

- **"Slow-and-go traffic"** or **"stop-and-go traffic"**: This is the default setting for many California freeways during

172

commute hours. It means you'll be doing a delightful dance between acceleration and braking, a vehicular waltz that tests your patience and your brake pads.

- **"Bumper-to-bumper"**: This is when "slow-and-go" seems like a distant, idyllic memory. It means you're essentially parked on the freeway, close enough to read the bumper stickers of the car in front of you (and silently judge their life choices).

- **"Gridlock"**: The ultimate traffic apocalypse. All movement ceases. Hope abandons you. This is when you start contemplating the feasibility of abandoning your car and starting a new life as a pedestrian.

- **"A stalled vehicle in the number 2 lane"**: Traffic reports are often very specific about which lane is affected. Lanes are typically numbered from left to right, with the far-left lane being the number 1 lane. Knowing this helps you visualize the blockage and strategize your (often futile) lane changes.

- **"Accident blocking the right shoulder"**: This might sound less dire, but don't be fooled. The ensuing "rubbernecking delay" or "lookie-loo slowdown" from curious drivers can back things up for miles.

- **"Metering lights are on"**: These are the traffic signals at freeway on-ramps, designed to regulate the flow of vehicles entering the freeway. When they're active, especially in the Bay Area and Los Angeles, it's a sign that the freeway is already struggling, and you'll have an extra wait just to get on.

- **"HOV lane"** or **"Carpool lane"**: High Occupancy Vehicle lanes are often a topic of discussion, especially if there's an incident blocking them or if someone is illegally using them. Reports might specify if restrictions are in effect (e.g., "2 or more persons per vehicle").

- **"Breakdown"**: A common term for any disabled vehicle, from a flat tire to an engine failure, causing a lane blockage and the inevitable delay.

- **"Overturned big rig"**: These are the multi-hour nightmares. An overturned truck, especially if it's carrying something messy or hazardous, can shut down lanes or entire sections of freeway for a very, very long time. If you hear this on your route, consider turning around and going back to bed.

- **"Debris in lanes"**: This can be anything from a stray ladder, a mattress, a shredded tire, or even, occasionally, livestock. Caltrans works to clear these, but not before they cause a bit of vehicular chaos.

- **"Traffic moving at the limit"**: This phrase is uttered with a certain hushed reverence, like spotting a unicorn. It means, miraculously, that things are flowing smoothly. Savor these moments; they are fleeting.

- **"The usual suspects"**: Reporters often refer to chronically congested freeways or interchanges by this moniker, acknowledging their daily contribution to commuter misery.

- **"Clearing the scene"**: This refers to the process of removing damaged vehicles, debris, and emergency responders after an incident. It's a slow, painstaking process that always feels like it takes longer than it should when you're stuck in the backup.

- **Specific interchange names**: You'll quickly learn the infamous local names for major freeway junctions, like "The El Toro Y" (where the I-5 and I-405 merge/split in Orange County), "The Orange Crush" (where the I-5, SR-22, and SR-57 converge in Orange County), or "The MacArthur Maze" (the complex interchange of I-80, I-580, and I-880 in Oakland). These are often hotspots for congestion and incidents.

Beyond the vocabulary, there's the **psychology of the traffic report**. It's a daily emotional rollercoaster. A surprisingly clear report can fill you with an almost giddy sense of hope, a feeling that you might actually make it to work on time and with your sanity intact. A bad report, full of SigAlerts and deep red lines on the map, can cast a pall over your entire morning, leading to strategic calculations of alternate routes, frantic texts to your boss, or simply a resigned sigh as you pour an extra-strong cup of coffee.

The traffic report also fuels the **"beat the traffic" game**, an eternal quest waged by millions of Californians. This involves trying to leave just early enough (or late enough) to avoid the worst of the congestion, or constantly searching for that mythical, undiscovered surface street shortcut that will shave precious minutes off your commute. Spoiler alert: that shortcut rarely exists, or if it does, Waze has already told everyone else about it.

For many, the final stage in their relationship with the traffic report is a kind of Zen-like **acceptance or resignation**. You check the report, you acknowledge the impending doom, and then you simply get in your car and join the slow-moving herd, armed with your podcasts, your audiobooks, and perhaps a well-developed repertoire of calming breathing exercises. You can't control the traffic, but you can (theoretically) control your reaction to it.

Using the information from a traffic report effectively is an art form. Do you trust the radio reporter who says your route is clear, or does your gut tell you that Waze's prediction of a 90-minute crawl is more accurate? Do you stick to the freeway and hope the accident clears quickly, or do you dive onto surface streets, risking a labyrinth of stoplights and school zones? There's no right answer, and even the best information can become outdated in minutes as new incidents occur. This unpredictability is part of what makes California traffic so uniquely... character-building.

The **personalities of traffic reporters** can also become part of the experience. Some are calm and reassuring, delivering news of utter gridlock with a soothing baritone. Others are more energetic, almost gleefully describing the chaos. Some develop catchphrases or on-air rivalries. They become familiar voices, guides through the daily transportation morass, and for many, an integral part of their commuting routine. There's a certain dark humor in hearing a reporter describe a 15-mile backup due to a single stalled car with an air of complete normalcy, because, well, it *is* normal here.

For some long-time Californians, the traffic report eventually fades into **white noise**, the background hum of a life lived in a very populous state. It's there, it's noted, but it no longer elicits the same emotional highs and lows. It's just another piece of information to be factored into the complex algorithm of daily existence. This level of stoicism is a hard-won achievement.

The California traffic report is more than just a list of delays; it's a reflection of the state's dynamism, its density, and its perpetual motion. It's a daily reminder that you are one of millions trying to get from point A to point B, often simultaneously. Learning to listen to it, understand its nuances, and perhaps even find a perverse sort of entertainment in its daily dispatches, is a rite of passage. It won't make the traffic disappear, unfortunately, but it might just make you feel a little more prepared, a little more informed, and a little more like a true Californian, sighing along with everyone else as you hear about that overturned big rig on the Grapevine. Now, if you'll excuse me, I think I just heard my freeway mentioned... and it wasn't good news.

CHAPTER TWENTY-FIVE:
Congratulations! You're (Almost) a Californian Now (Here's What's Next)

Well, would you look at that? You've wrestled with the hydra of California bureaucracy, navigated freeways that sometimes resemble abstract performance art, and perhaps even learned to distinguish your artisanal kale from your everyday lawn clippings. You've read the preceding twenty-four chapters (or at least skimmed them while hyperventilating about housing costs). You might have boxes (mostly) unpacked, a semi-permanent address, and a growing suspicion that "sunshine tax" isn't just a cute phrase. Congratulations are in order! You've made it. You're here. You are, for all intents and purposes, a Californian-in-progress. The keyword here, dear friend, is "progress."

Becoming a Californian isn't like flipping a switch or crossing a state line. There's no official ceremony where they hand you a surfboard and a lifetime supply of avocados (though wouldn't that be something?). It's a slow burn, a gradual assimilation, a process more akin to marinating than microwaving. You've handled the initial onslaught – the move, the DMV, the job hunt. Now comes the long game: truly settling in and understanding what it means to live in this beautifully bewildering, perpetually perplexing, and undeniably unique corner of the world. This isn't about more hurdles to jump, but rather about the evolving landscape of your new life.

One of the first things you might notice is a subtle shift in your own perspective. Things that once seemed utterly bizarre – say, a menu dedicated entirely to different types of toast, or a casual conversation about earthquake preparedness kits – will start to feel... normal. The sheer scale of the state, which once felt daunting, might begin to feel more manageable as you carve out your own familiar routes and routines. That initial culture shock, the feeling of being an outsider looking in, will gradually fade, replaced by a quiet understanding of the local rhythms.

You'll also develop a deeper appreciation for what we might call "California Patience," a specialized form of forbearance that extends beyond just traffic jams. It's the patience required to wait for a table at that perpetually packed brunch spot, the patience to navigate the byzantine online portal for your kid's school fundraiser, the patience to understand that "just around the corner" can mean a 45-minute drive in LA. This isn't resignation; it's a pragmatic adaptation, a recognition that some things here simply move at their own, often glacial, pace.

Now that you're no longer just a wide-eyed newcomer, you might find yourself more attuned to the ongoing civic life of the Golden State. California politics is a spectator sport, a full-contact engagement, and occasionally, a source of profound bewilderment for even long-term residents. Get ready for ballot propositions. Oh, the glorious, numerous, and often incredibly complex ballot propositions. Every election cycle, you'll be presented with a booklet (often the size of a small novel) detailing proposed laws on everything from school bonds to environmental regulations to who-knows-what-they'll-think-of-next. Deciphering these requires dedication, research, and perhaps a strong cup of coffee.

Local elections for city council, school boards, and various special districts also carry significant weight, directly impacting your daily life. And community involvement, whether it's attending a town hall meeting, volunteering for a local cause (as we nudged you towards in Chapter Fourteen), or simply engaging in spirited (but hopefully civil) debate with your neighbors about the new bike lane proposal, is a very Californian way to participate in the democratic process. You are, after all, paying for it (Chapter Twenty-Three says hello).

Remember that initial bureaucratic gauntlet you ran? The DMV, the utility companies, the endless forms? Well, the fun doesn't stop there, it just becomes more… intermittent. Renewing your driver's license, your vehicle registration (annually, with that delightful Vehicle License Fee), or any professional licenses you might hold will become recurring blips on your administrative radar. If you decide to undertake any home improvement projects, even seemingly minor ones, you'll reacquaint yourself with the joys of local planning departments and the permit process, which in some California jurisdictions, has been known to outlast presidential administrations. Keeping good records, and an even better sense of humor, remains essential.

Water consciousness, which you hopefully embraced upon arrival, will likely transition from a "new thing I have to do" to an ingrained habit. You'll find yourself instinctively taking shorter showers, eyeing your neighbor's lush green lawn with a mixture of suspicion and envy (depending on current drought conditions), and perhaps even developing strong opinions on the best type of drought-tolerant groundcover. Understanding where your local water comes from, the complexities of California's water rights system, and the ongoing efforts to ensure a sustainable water future can become a surprisingly engaging topic of conversation, especially if you want to sound like a seasoned local.

Beyond just sorting your trash into the correct bins (Chapter Ten, we're still proud of you), the broader environmental ethos of California will likely permeate your daily choices. You might find yourself scrutinizing product packaging for its recyclability, opting for brands that emphasize sustainability, or feeling a subtle societal nudge to reduce your carbon footprint. From debates about renewable energy sources to efforts to protect California's stunning coastline and vast wilderness areas, environmentalism isn't just a niche interest here; it's a mainstream concern that often influences policy, consumer behavior, and even social interactions.

One of the defining characteristics of California is its relentless pursuit of the "new." This is the land of innovation, of disruption, of constantly asking "what's next?" This isn't just confined to the tech bubbles of Silicon Valley or Silicon Beach. You'll see it in evolving culinary trends, new forms of artistic expression, shifting social norms, and an endless parade of startups promising to revolutionize everything from dog walking to space travel. This constant churn can be exciting, keeping life interesting and pushing boundaries. It can also be exhausting, making it feel like you're perpetually trying to catch up with the latest app, the newest slang, or the most current wellness fad (Chapter Twenty-Two sends its regards).

So, how do you know if you're truly starting to meld into the Californian landscape? There are subtle tells, little indicators that you're no longer just visiting. You might find yourself:

- Giving directions to a lost tourist, not just with accuracy, but with a certain weary authority, perhaps even throwing in a tip about avoiding the 405 between 3 PM and 7 PM.

- Having a deeply entrenched, non-negotiable opinion on the best local taco truck, and being willing to defend its honor with surprising passion.

- Experiencing a minor earthquake tremor (a "roller," as some call them) and your first instinct is to glance at the light fixtures to see how much they're swaying, rather than immediately diving under the nearest piece of flimsy furniture.

- Referring to Karl the Fog by name, or discussing the Santa Ana winds not as a weather phenomenon, but as a malevolent entity that messes with your sinuses and your mood.

- No longer audibly gasping when you see the price of a small basket of organic blueberries at the farmers market. You might still wince internally, but the gasp is gone.

- Complaining about the traffic, not with the shocked outrage of a newcomer, but with the resigned, almost poetic bitterness of a long-suffering veteran. Bonus points if you have a preferred alternate route that you believe is a closely guarded secret.

- Automatically reaching for your reusable shopping bags before you even leave the house, and feeling a pang of shame if you forget them.

- Understanding that "beach weather" in San Francisco often means a sweater and a windbreaker, while "beach weather" in San Diego means sunscreen and a prayer for parking.

As you settle in, you'll also likely develop your own version of the California Paradox: that complex, often contradictory, relationship many residents have with the state. You might find yourself simultaneously adoring the breathtaking natural beauty and lamenting the crowds that flock to enjoy it. You might champion the state's progressive ideals while groaning under the weight of its taxes and regulations. You might curse the cost of living one day and then feel an immense sense of gratitude for a perfect sunset over the Pacific the next. It's okay. Loving California and being occasionally infuriated by it are not mutually exclusive emotions; they're practically a package deal.

So, what's next for you, the (almost) Californian? The initial whirlwind of moving and setting up is largely behind you. Now begins the deeper, more nuanced work of building a life here. It's about continuing to explore, not just the famous landmarks, but the hidden corners of your own neighborhood, the diverse communities within your region, and the vast landscapes that lie beyond your usual commute. It's about staying curious, being open to new experiences, and remaining adaptable in a state that is defined by its constant evolution.

Your California story is still being written, by you. The preceding chapters have hopefully provided a roadmap, some practical advice, and perhaps a few laughs to help you navigate the initial terrain. But the ongoing journey, the process of truly making this place your own, is a uniquely personal one. There will be challenges, undoubtedly. There will be moments of frustration, certainly. But there will also be moments of incredible beauty, unexpected joy, and profound connection that will remind you why you embarked on this adventure in the first place.

California isn't just a place you move to; it's a place you continually engage with, a place that shapes you even as you find your own way to shape your experience within it. So, keep that adventurous spirit alive. Keep learning, keep exploring, and keep embracing the glorious, frustrating, and utterly unique tapestry that is life in the Golden State. You've got this. Mostly. And if all else fails, at least you know how to complain about the traffic like a pro. Welcome, (almost) Californian. The next chapter is yours to write.

Made in United States
North Haven, CT
20 August 2025